EXPLAINING SCIENCE IN THE CLASSROOM

Jon Ogborn
Gunther Kress
Isabel Martins
Kieran McGillicuddy

OPEN UNIVERSITY PRESS
Buckingham · Philadelphia

Open University Press
Celtic Court
22 Ballmoor
Buckingham
MK18 1XW

and
1900 Frost Road, Suite 101
Bristol, PA 19007, USA

First Published 1996

A catalogue record of this book is available from the British Library

ISBN   0 335 19720 5 (hb)   0 335 19719 1 (pb)

Library of Congress Cataloging-in-Publication Data
Explaining science in the classroom / Jon Ogborn . . . [et al.]
        p. cm.
    Includes bibliographical references and index.
    ISBN 0-335-19720-5   ISBN 0-335-19719-1 (pbk)
    1. Science—Study and teaching (Secondary)   2. Semiotics.
I. Ogborn, Jon.
Q181.E87   1996
507'.12—dc20   96-13433
                                                            CIP

Typeset by Graphicraft Typesetters Ltd, Hong Kong
Printed in Great Britain by St Edmundsbury Press,
Bury St Edmunds, Suffolk

CONTENTS

PREFACE

This book is one of the products of collaborative research between science education and semiotics and discourse analysis at the University of London Institute of Education. It is addressed to all those concerned with the teaching of science – to science teachers and to those who train or advise them.

We started this work in the belief that science education had much to learn from those who study language, meaning and communication, an area which may be subsumed under the label 'semiotics' – the study of the making of meaning. We also hoped that the teaching of science would prove to be a fruitful field for investigation by semioticians, offering them new challenges and requiring new insights. In the event, we believe that both of these hopes have been realized, at least, they have for us. Not only has the collaboration led to the results described here, but it has also led us to further collaboration, currently on the use of images in science. And we will want to follow up the implications of the work which was started here.

The book is based on video-tapes of a number of secondary school teachers explaining science. The argument of the book is copiously illustrated with transcripts taken from these recordings. This generates two problems of which the reader should be made aware. One is that language – 'the words' – is thereby given prominence over other modes of communication, because there are no easy ways of representing all the non-verbal communication which is present. We have tried to offset this partially by including in the transcripts commentary on actions, gestures, writing, pointing and doing things with apparatus, etc. The second problem is that speech does not transcribe in any simple way into the normal forms of written language. Nothing, for example, corresponds in speech to the full stop in writing (just as nothing in writing corresponds to the intonation which says, 'Don't interrupt me yet, I haven't finished'). We decided, at the risk of annoying our friends in linguistics, to present the transcripts in a way which would make them as easy as possible for the science teacher, untrained in linguistic notations, to read. Thus we have used some of the devices of written language to assist the reader to grasp the essential sense of what was said with the minimum effort.

We have used the following notations and conventions in transcripts:

- Full stops (.) and capitalizing initial letters of new sentences are used to create a 'written' version of the speech, where the speech without them would be tiresome or puzzling to read. We have done this – that is, using conventions of writing to represent speech – as sparingly as possible. Colons and semicolons are occasionally used for this purpose too.
- Dashes (–) indicate places where the speaker abandons one way of expressing something and starts again, or where an aside is inserted. A dash is also used for an uncompleted word (for example, 'Hen–' where a speaker might start to address 'Henry' but then switches to another name).
- Commas (,) indicate places where the listener feels a pause, even if there is no actual pause, because an idea is being extended or repeated. Sometimes there will be an audible pause.
- Question marks (?), used at the end of an utterance or after a word (e.g. 'OK?') indicate a questioning intonation. A question is being asked or implied.
- [ ] indicates a noticeable pause or hesitation, longer than those of the speaker's habitual rhythms.
- [?] symbolizes a device quite often used by teachers – a hanging questioning space at the end of an utterance, which expects an answer which would complete the utterance (as in 'So this is called a [?]').
- Comments in italics in square brackets describe non-linguistic acts of communication (for example [*teacher writes on blackboard*]), at approximately the place in the speech at which they occur, but placed so as to break up the spoken text into more or less intelligible units.
- Three dots (. . .) indicate elisions from the recording, placed in the text when the same speaker continues, and in the place for the speaker's identity where a speaker has been elided.
- Where turns to speak are taken normally, each speaker's text begins with a capital letter. Where one person interrupts another, and they talk at once, we break off the first speaker's transcript without a final punctuation, insert the interruption as if a new speaker had taken over, and then continue the first speaker's words but without an initial capital letter.
- A special pace and intonation is used when dictating or when giving something particular emphasis. We have not tried to represent this textually, but have added notes in parentheses to indicate where it occurs. Words 'spelt out' are printed with spaced characters.
- Very occasionally, we use italic type to indicate the stress, where there is otherwise ambiguity (for example, '*I* do' versus 'I *do*').
- The teachers are identified by pseudonyms, which remain the same through-

out the book. Thus the 'David' of Chapter 1 is the same 'David' who appears in Chapter 7, but his real name is not David. Students are also given pseudonyms where the teacher uses a name, and are identified by that pseudonym when they speak. Otherwise, student speakers are identified as 'Student', using 'Student 1', 'Student 2', etc. where it is necessary to keep track of who said what in a series of exchanges. We use 'Students' as identifying the speaker(s) when more than one student says the same thing. The pseudonyms preserve gender and ethnicity.

- Just occasionally, for our own purposes, we want to highlight a section of transcript. In this case, the relevant part of the transcript is set in ***bold italics***.

We decided not to burden the main text of the book with references to other work. Instead, we offer at the end of the book an Appendix which lists and briefly discusses the main sources on which we have drawn, putting them in context and adding references to further reading which may be of use.

We hope that this book represents a useful new departure in science education. In recent years, attention has been focused very strongly on students and their understandings of science and of the world around them. Learning science has been seen very largely as a problem for students, and especially so the more learning has been understood as an active process of the learner. We do not want to go back on that commitment to the need for learners to make knowledge their own, but we do want to open up a space for teachers to be thought about as having more to do than creating good conditions for learning. To teach is to act on other minds, which may then react as well as acting for themselves. So what teachers do in this way is worth describing and understanding. What we hope to have provided is the beginning of a new language for thinking about the act of explaining science in the classroom.

ACKNOWLEDGEMENTS

The research was done with the support of the Economic and Social Research Council, grant R000234916; support which we hereby gratefully acknowledge.

It was of course the group of teachers who so willingly agreed to have their lessons recorded, often on several occasions, who made this work possible at all. To Bob Chandler, Chris Gleeson, Shirley Kirk, Ian Hogg, Wendy di Marco, Eugene McConlough, Ogugua Okolo, Jenny Richardson, Will Fell, Phillipa Thompson, Mike Vingoe and Rob Walker we offer our thanks for their practical help, for their willingness to allow themselves to be observed and recorded, and for the many helpful discussions we had with them. We also gratefully acknowledge the assistance given by their schools: Swakeley's School for Girls, North Westminster School, Riddlesdown High School and Harris City Technology College.

We thank those colleagues from our own and other universities who joined us for a very useful critical two-day seminar part way through the project. We have drawn gratefully on ideas embodied in various unpublished manuscripts by Theo van Leeuwen, Mick O'Donnell and Robert Veel. We thank Nicolaos Christodoulou for helpful discussions and for giving us access to his data, Hugh Dunlop for interesting discussions, and Jenny Frost for her many insightful comments on the manuscript of the book. We thank Judy Benstead for her unstinting and efficient secretarial help during the preparation of the manuscript.

Chapter 1

CLASSROOMS, EXPLAINING AND SCIENCE

Who are *we*?

This book has been written by an unusual combination of people, coming from science education and from studies of communication. It seems obvious that this is a good collaboration to have if you are interested in how things are explained in the science classroom. There is, however, little tradition of bringing science education and studies of language together, even though independently people within science education have thought about language and people interested in communication and discourse have thought about science. Work starting from science education is in danger of using too limited a model of how language and communication works. And work starting from language is in danger of not grasping the sources of difficulty and the structuring of scientific ideas.

We have tried not merely to add the two points of view together, but to make them interact, to reach a synthesis neither could achieve without the other. As a result, our notions of what it is to explain scientific ideas have changed, and so too have some of our thoughts about what is important in language and communication more generally. This book is one outcome. It is mainly addressed to those interested in problems of teaching science. But we hope it will also be of interest more widely, to anyone concerned with understanding language and communication.

What is there to understand about explaining science?

Nearly every science teacher would agree that explaining things is fundamental to a science teacher's job. It is not of course the whole job, but it is a central and crucial part of it. Students whose teachers 'don't explain properly' get restive. And there is a lot of explaining to do. Why can metal ships float even though metals sink? How do we catch colds? What keeps the Moon going round the Earth? How does the fizz get into fizzy drinks? How do plants grow? What is the 'greenhouse effect' and does it matter? Where do the colours of soap bubbles come from? What happens to salt or sugar when they dissolve in water? What is rust and where does it come from? What are plastics made of? And so on, indefinitely.

The pages of science teachers' journals, such as the *School Science Review*, are full of explanations. Many of them are in the form of demonstrations or experiments to do. The assumption is that if the teacher arranges for an effect to be clearly seen, it will be clearly understood. But we all know that this is not true. We show the atmosphere crushing a tin can as air is removed from it, but the class sees the vacuum pump 'sucking' the sides of the can together. We show an electric current going round a circuit and they see electricity used up to 'make' the light from a lamp.

There are also theoretical things to explain. Teachers have to explain that it is the ceaseless motion of molecules which gives a gas its pressure, and which accounts for the energy we call 'heat'. They have to explain that plants build their tissue using carbon dioxide, water and sunlight. They have to explain that chemical equilibrium is really a dynamic two-way process of change in both directions at once – that it only *seems* to be a case of nothing happening at all.

Finally, and hardest of all, science teachers have to explain things that do not seem to need explaining at all. How do we see things? Why are our bodies warm? Why does coal burn? Why do hot things cool down? Why is the sky dark at night? Why do mammals have four limbs? Why are solids hard and liquids runny? Such things seem to common sense to be so obvious that there is no need to explain them. Indeed, nobody asks how to explain them because they are just the kind of thing we *use to explain other things*. Why shake the foundations unnecessarily? And yet it is typical of the sciences that they do shake the foundations of knowledge in this way.

The act and art of explaining to a class is much less discussed than the scientific ideas to be explained. Of course teachers swap ideas with one another, often about useful analogies and models. But *explaining* is not treated as something which could be understood, learned or taught. What can be said about it is mainly anecdotal, lacking any systematic or thought-out basis. Beginning teachers are supposed to learn by example how to explain, often without being conscious of doing so; experience is taken to be the only possible teacher. There is no body of evidence on which to base arguments about how explaining can be done, and what different ways there are of doing it. There is no shared theory of what is involved in explaining. Above all, there is no common language for talking about explaining, except for such common-sense terms as 'clear' or 'confusing', 'complicated' or 'simple'. We hope in this book to provide the beginnings of such a language to describe and compare different cases of explaining in the science classroom. And of course we hope that this language will prove useful to some teachers of subjects other than science.

Our work has had two different kinds of outcome: practical and theoretical. The practical outcomes are ways of thinking about explaining very different topics and ideas in science – such as the periodic table and the nature of sound – which allow them to be compared or contrasted. Thus practising teachers get new tools for thinking about what they are doing.

The theoretical outcomes are ways of linking the highly specific job of explaining scientific ideas to broader issues in communication. Explaining science can now be seen in a larger perspective, which takes on board how language, action, gesture and personal relations come together in acts of communication. But also, theories of communication are not left unchanged. In particular, they have to take account of the way science is not just about words but is also about things.

Explaining: some examples

We will now briefly offer a few examples of explaining going on in the science classroom, to illustrate the kinds of things we found we needed to take into account. Here is a teacher (David) explaining the digestive system to a Year 10 class:

> *David*: Now, the tube that goes through the middle of the worm, is [ ] The tube that goes through the middle of the worm is actually connected to the outside world. Here's the outside world here, here's the outside world here, and the tube going through the middle is part of the outside, of the outside world. It's not actually part of the worm, it's just a hole going through the middle. Let me put it to you another way. You know packs of Polo mints, yeah? You know if you buy a pack of Polo mints they look like this – and then you unwrap them, and you find that this Polo mint looks like this up to the top here, when you take the top Polo mint off and you eat it. But in the middle of the Polo mint there's a hole, yeah?, and if you've got a packet of Polo mints then that hole goes in and out the other end. Now – is the hole part of the Polo mint or not?

The first thing to notice is that the words on the page are not enough. The teacher had a diagram on the blackboard which is an essential part of the explanation. Figure 1.1 shows more or less what it looked like, in all its stark simplicity. The diagram, and gestures involving it, are all part of the explanation. So is the imagined tube of Polo mints. The way David is making meanings goes well beyond language. Of course what he says is important, but spoken language is just one of a number of meaning systems which are in use.

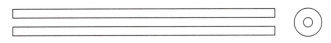

Figure 1.1 An earthworm brutally reduced to essentials

Secondly, the earthworm pictured here is like no recognizable earthworm. Indeed, this teacher is not really discussing earthworms at all. He is working towards the fundamental but – from the point of view of people's everyday feelings about their bodies – bizarre idea that our digestive insides are open to the outside. The strange diagram is a diagram, not of an earthworm but of the geometry of digestion. David is making the familiar and comfortable become strange. A new way of thinking about organisms as topological objects is being developed. This is another constant theme in our work – the need in explaining to make parts of the world new and unfamiliar, and to re-imagine what had until then seemed familiar and obvious. To explain, things have to be transformed, sometimes radically.

Thirdly, the explanation works by opening up a gap of understanding needing to be filled – a feeling of a difference of view needing to be resolved. To refer to such a picture as an earthworm is to create such a difference. There is a tension, deliberately created, between what is said and what is seen. As a result, there is clearly something to explain. Much of our work has looked at the different ways in which science teachers create the need for explanations.

Fourthly, the Polo mints serve as an analogy. We have found it necessary to look at the way science teachers continually transform ideas through metaphor and analogy. Indeed, the transformation of knowledge in various ways, transformations both of scientific ideas into representations which work in the classroom, and transformations of ideas within the classroom, form a major theme of our work.

Fifthly, this explanation is not isolated. It comes from somewhere and it is going somewhere. It will develop into a more detailed account of how digestion works in a variety of organisms, and also into a more generalized account of digestive 'systems' as a whole. Explanations in science classrooms cannot be understood without seeing how they fit into larger scale explanations, whilst also often themselves containing explanations (as this example contains the Polo mint analogy). They exist on many time scales all at once. Another example is the following, in which near the start of a series of Year 10 lessons on the chemical periodic table a teacher (Ruth) tries to explain why the periodic table is important:

> *Ruth*: And the periodic table – I think is a wonder. And I think it really does help you understand chemistry much easier than anything else really. Now chemistry is an exceedingly easy subject, and why it's easy is because it's full of sense – common sense and logic.

Within this large-scale explanation, which previews three lessons, there are many subsidiary explanations, for example of the division of the periodic table into metals and non-metals:

Ruth: Metals always lose electrons and non-metals always gain electrons. So if you take Group I . . . going down they've all got one electron in the outer shell and when they combine with another element they lose their electron and give it to another atom.

Explanations exist right down to the smallest scale, for example of how to read the data in one cell of the periodic table:

Ruth: . . . the bottom number tells you how many protons there are in the nucleus of the atom.

What we have to look at are structures of explanations, not just individual bits of explanation.

So far in these examples we have not heard from students. This is not to say that the students were not thinking, nor that the teacher was excluding them. The explaining going on was obviously highly tuned to their concerns and knowledge. David links his surprising view of digestion to something very familiar. Ruth uses the students' concern with learning being made easier to try to engage them in the work to come.

Teacher and students talking together can also construct explanations. A common form of interaction, often described in other work such as John Sinclair and Malcolm Coulthard's *Towards an Analysis of Discourse*, is the triad 'question–answer–evaluation', as in the following example:

Elaine: Which of these things on the periodic table might be joined together to make hydrocarbons?
Student: Hydrogen.
Elaine: Hydrogen and [?]
Student: Carbon.
Elaine: Carbon, right. These are compounds of hydrogen and carbon.

Elaine clearly evaluates the response 'carbon'. She also evaluates the response 'hydrogen' by indicating that there is more to come, making this her next question.

In other cases, students make more of the running and are led into suggesting explanations (sometimes competing ones), drawing on what they know or can imagine. This is difficult to illustrate briefly, because it involves an extended to and fro of discussion. But here is a taste of one example, discussed further later in Chapter 7. The teacher, Leon, and his Year 10 class are thinking about what might be needed in joints in the skeleton to stop the bones wearing away as the joint moves. Leon is in the middle of getting the class to 'design a joint':

Leon: Let's try and stop the wearing away. How can we stop the wearing away? Emma, how can we stop the wearing away?
Emma: [*Inaudible*]
Leon: Yes?
Emma: Put a sheet of something between it.
Leon: Yeah, what sort of sheet?
Student: Tissues.

Student: No, no, that'd be like,
Leon: That's rough isn't it.
Student: [*Inaudible*]
Student: I know.
Student: Perhaps an elastic band.
Student: No, a flat sheet, between 'em, a disc or something.
Leon: And what would the disc do, instead of rubbing on– ?
Student: It'd stop them hitting each other.
Leon: So instead of rubbing on each other they're rubbing on this, like, plastic thing?
Student: Yeah, but they . . .
Student: Fluids, like fluids, yeah.
Leon: Some sort of, what would fluids do though?
Students: [*Talking all together*]
Student: They stop 'em rubbing it.
Leon: Like oil.
Student: But your weight'd be moving, your weight'd be doing that [*gestures*].
Leon: Like oil?
Student: Like oil, like they show it in the car advert.

Clearly the students are involved in constructing ideas. But in David's class they may well have puzzled silently about whether humans really are just digestive tubes, and in Elaine's class may have wondered whether the mess and variety of chemical elements can really be organized so tidily. Thus we have had to think about how explanations could activate students' knowledge, ideas and imaginations, without always having overt evidence of it happening.

We also notice the importance of material things in scientific explanations. These material things are certainly things 'out there', existing in the material world as cartilage exists in joints. But at the same time they are meaningful and 'made' – the result of cultural work produced by particular people for particular reasons. 'Joints' exist all right, and when one gets arthritis one knows it. But they are also a biological category, having a small number of general types, and related to the 'design' of body plans of vertebrates (a subtext of Leon's lesson). They are part of the biologist's kit of parts for thinking with. We could say the same for genes, electrons or carbohydrates.

With these examples, we have introduced several of the main themes of the book. In the remainder of this chapter we will discuss more generally the ideas on which we have relied, and the theoretical framework we have developed for describing explanation in the science classroom.

Where do *we* come from?

We are not of course the first to express an interest in explanations, or in science classrooms. But previous work has tended to focus either on explanations as such (whether in science, or more generally as in Charles Antaki's book *Analysing Everyday Explanation*) or on language in the classroom.

It has been common to think of classroom talk in science as 'inducting students into scientific discourse' – as their learning to 'talk science'. We treat the same issues as a matter of how 'entities of science' are brought into being for students. This reflects our preference for going beyond the realm of words and what they refer to, to stress the role played by action, real and imagined, by and on material things. And we extend this preference to conceptual, meaning-carrying, semiotic 'things'. This view is inspired by some current philosophy of science, particular Rom Harré's *Varieties of Realism* and Roy Bhaskar's *A Realist Theory of Science*. We take from them the idea of explanation as resting on 'how things are', as being stories about how a set of entities can produce the phenomenon to be explained. This conception makes space for analogy and metaphor in explanation, often driven by implicit even unconscious metaphors. Here we draw on work such as Eleanor Rosch and Barbara Lloyd's *Cognition and Categorization*, and George Lakoff's book about the metaphorical basis of thinking, *Women, Fire and Dangerous Things*.

We also arrive here influenced by the later work of Jean Piaget on the construction of meaning through action. In his later work on the logic of meanings, Piaget offers an account of how the meanings of entities are constructed through action, through what they can do, what you can do to them and what they are made of (what parts they have). A valuable source, besides Piaget's earlier work, has been his posthumously published book with Rolando Garcia, *Toward a Logic of Meaning*.

Much discussion about problems in science teaching has revolved around the role of practical activity in the classroom – of 'doing and understanding'. Clive Sutton's more recent work on the language of science, in *Words, Science and Learning*, represents a well-articulated and richly illustrated argument for a necessary change of focus. His inspection of the 'language of science' from the point of view of a science educator traces the metaphorical origin of scientific terms which are nowadays taken for granted ('cells' for example). He provides a plethora of examples of the way scientists' choice of words is part of their understanding and interpreting of phenomena. By choice he pays attention mainly just to words, wanting teachers to focus on them as active interpretations rather than as passive labels.

At the larger scales of clause and of text, the linguists Michael Halliday and Jim Martin in their book *Writing Science* analyse the grammar of scientific discourse. They note how the strikingly 'dense' nature of scientific writing is achieved through what they call 'grammatical metaphor'. In this, a whole physical process is condensed into a single entity, for example, 'the bending of light as it enters a transparent material such as glass or water is called *refraction*'. A process becomes a noun, and the text typically goes on to talk about refraction and to use it in further relationships. Density quickly builds up, as in, 'Developments in hand may lead to variable-speed turbines and improved aerofoils that yield greater efficiency', to take an only modestly dense example. We see this, however, as much more than simply a question of writing and grammatical structure – much more than just a special way of talking. We see it as building new and different views of the world.

Halliday and Martin have identified 'report' and 'explanation' as different genres of scientific texts. We argue instead that scientific explanations rely at bottom on what things are and what they can do, generating stories about how things can have acted together to account for some phenomenon. Here the influence of the later work of Piaget and Garcia on our thinking about how meanings are constructed through action is evident.

A linguistic starting point very naturally leads to seeing learning science as learning scientific terms and how they are related. For example, in his *Talking Science*, Jay Lemke sees the student's job of understanding the teacher's explanations as one of identifying thematic patterns and grasping semantic relations between words. This may give undue importance to language, especially in the case of science where we see much meaning being made through acting on things and doing things with them.

Others, particularly Derek Edwards and Neil Mercer in *Common Knowledge*, have been clear that the language in the classroom is by no means everything that matters – 'Overt messages, things actually said, are only a small part of communication' (p. 160). They rightly look at the negotiation of shared meanings and assumptions. We have tried to go further, and to look at all the activity of the classroom – talk, gesture, pictures, graphs and tables, experimenting, doing demonstrations – as ways of making meanings. We are also not sure about their idea of the goal being achieving 'common knowledge' through teacher and student pooling experience and knowledge, though this must and can play a part (as in the example above about joints). The relation between teacher and pupil is surely much more asymmetrical. For this reason we rely more on a notion of semiotic 'difference' or 'tension' driving explanation, as suggested above in the example of the earthworm.

Our theoretical framework: an overview

The main outcome of our work is a language for describing explanations in the science classroom. This language does not tell you what is 'good' or 'bad', what is effective or ineffective. What it does is to offer a way of thinking about what explanations are, when and why they are felt to be needed, what constructing an explanation involves, how explanations transform knowledge, and different 'styles' in which explaining can be done. This section merely outlines these ideas. The purpose of the whole book is to illustrate and elaborate them.

Our theoretical framework – our language for describing explanations – has three main components:

- scientific explanations as analogous to 'stories'
- an account of meaning-making in explanation, itself with four main parts:
  creating differences
  constructing entities

transforming knowledge
putting meaning into matter
• variation and styles of explanation

We now offer brief accounts of each; these will serve the reader as a guide to the book, and as a foretaste of what it has to offer.

Scientific explanation

What makes a scientific explanation be something that *explains*? If I ask why it is raining and you tell me that water is falling from the sky, I have been told only what raining *is*. If you tell me that it is raining because it rains a lot in April, I have been told only that raining is usual and needs no further explanation. But a story about a depression coming across the Atlantic and bringing wet air with it begins to do the job. Such an explanation tells how something or other comes about. This makes a scientific explanation very much like a story, even though it may not be told like a story. Some vital features of a story are that:

• there is a cast of protagonists, each of which has its own capabilities which are what makes it what it is
• members of this cast enact one of the many series of events of which they are capable
• these events have a consequence, which follows from the nature of the protagonists and the events they happened to enact

Let us in this light consider some examples of scientific explanations:

• how a river came to be polluted
• the origin of coal
• the transmission of disease
• the mechanism of heredity
• how television works

The explanation of how a river came to be polluted might be that farmers fertilize their crops, that rain washes fertilizer into the river, that the fertilizer makes plants in the water grow rapidly so that the water becomes full of decaying matter. The cast is farmers, fertilizers, rain, plants, etc. The story depends on knowing what fertilizers can do to plants, what rain can do to fertilizers, what plants do, and what rivers can do to decaying matter. Most of the things in the story are familiar.

An explanation of the origin of coal also uses common knowledge, but the story extends over hundreds of millions of years; ancient tropical forests, the laying down of sediment over decayed vegetation, the effects of extreme pressure and temperature. It may involve subsidiary less common-sensical stories of continents drifting and rocks folding. The need for scales of time outside any possible experience demands imagination to think of the explanation as what 'really happened'. The existence of an explanation makes a difference to what counts as a phenomenon. A mountain range dividing two countries is one thing; the mountain range as a case of a currently rising piece of the Earth's crust is another. The explanation tells us afresh what it is relevant to look for; what to see things as.

Since Pasteur, we live with a new world of invisible microscopic agents – bacteria and viruses. Although bacteria are visible in the microscope, explanations about them involve belief in a world, just as real as the everyday world, but on a scale too small to see or act upon directly.

An explanation of the mechanism of heredity introduces novel actions of novel entities. A mother and father passing characteristics to their child turns into a story about a molecule, DNA, which can make copies of itself. Possessing blue eyes or brown hair becomes possessing a set of chemically coded sequences in DNA. The story involves unfamiliar objects which do unfamiliar things in an inaccessible world.

With an explanation of the working of television we are again in the realm of unfamiliar new imagined entities – magnetic and electric fields. They seem real enough as they deliver the news bulletins, but when we ask what they are, the answers seem less than satisfying: 'A field is a region of space in which a force can act on a particle.' How could such a thing travel from studio to home? Fields, talked of as existing in the real world, are also clearly something which someone once just thought of, a construction of the mind.

It is clear that scientific explanations rely on the existence of worlds of protagonists whose possible behaviours make up the story. But it is also clear that these worlds of protagonists are often far from everyday common sense. Such explanations make no sense until we know what the entities involved are supposed to be able to do or have done to them.

A story tells how events work out so that the result is no longer arbitrary; so that it *makes sense*, so that what happens arises from things doing what it is in their nature to do. The 'nature of things', their meaning to us, is just what they can do, what can be done to them, and what they are made of. We have a sense of obviousness when we envisage events working out as they must because of how things are. And this is where explaining stops. When that is how things *are*.

Within scientific thinking, however, some unexpected things are treated as obvious. If you have a cold you must have been infected; that you were out in the rain on a chilly day is beside the point. And things which were once obvious can become obsolete and be replaced by quite different other things. For example, since Newton it is 'obvious' that a planet must go on travelling around its Sun for ever without having anything to keep its motion going; before Newton and still today in everyday common sense, 'obviously' any moving object must be kept moving by some cause.

In one important respect scientific explanations are *not* much like imaginative tales. Some of the best fictions create a closed world within which everything fits together imaginatively. Scientific explanations, by contrast, insist that their protagonists are to be taken as real things, existing beyond the closed world of one story. Germs are not to be thought of just as 'what causes disease'. If they exist, we want to know where they live and how they work. Taking something to be real means taking it to act as it does independently of our thinking and wishes. We cannot wish things into existence in one context and out of existence in another, as it suits us. And as we get more confident of the reality of imagined entities, the more we can act on them or get them to act on other things.

Scientific explanations also rely on formal, sometimes mathematical, constructions. Thus the protagonists in explanation-stories must also be thought of as including such entities as harmonic motion, rates of change, differential coefficients, exponential decay, negative feedback, vectors, and so on.

It may seem artificial to treat these formal entities on a par with material entities. Are they not just part of the law-like patterns of behaviour of material entities? The answer is that formal entities may begin life as law-like patterns, but often develop a life of their own in explanations. One example obvious to chemists is the case of 'orbitals' in atoms, treated in explanations of chemical bonding as entities with their own properties and powers, not merely as convenient pictures representing some arrangement of electrons. An 'ecological niche' is a formal metaphor used as if it were a real place to live, feed and be protected. Fields, once mathematical fictions, have become active real entities in their own right, storing energy and transmitting information. In modern particle physics, they are perhaps more real even than matter, which in common-sense mood we take as the paradigm of the real.

Creating differences

Nobody simply talks just for talking's sake, even if that is how it seems at times. Conversations seem to be merely casual, informal, inconsequential, usually pleasurable exchange; very little seems to be at issue. Certainly there should be no attempt to dominate. If this begins to happen, other participants feel uneasy and may comment on the shift from conversation: 'Don't start lecturing me!'; or 'I don't want to have an argument!'; or 'Don't be so serious!'

These responses indicate that even though they *feel* spontaneous and informal, conversations are circumscribed by rules – which become noticeable when they are broken. Rules of turn taking, topic change, interruption, or pausing while still holding the floor, have been extensively studied. Such rules are quite numerous, stable, and strictly observed by participants. Children have to learn them, and until they do find it difficult to join in a conversation.

In our view, the fundamental motor of communication is that there is something known to one participant and not – or often *assumed* not to be – known to another. I have something to say to you, which I think – or pretend – you do not know, and this allows me to open a conversation. There is a *difference* between us. It may be a difference of knowledge or information. It may be a difference of interest – perhaps I want to inform you of, or recruit you to, my interest. It may be a difference of status and power, which I want to acknowledge by being polite to you, or which I want to impress on you by obliging you to be polite to me. The difference may be in the realm of feeling: I may want you to know that I feel fondly towards you, or simply to let you know that there is no problem between us; and communication ensues – even if only briefly – in order to bridge this difference. The bridging of difference, dealing with it, is what drives communication.

Conversely, where there is no difference, there is no communication. Another metaphor for the same thing is that of *semiotic tension*. The existence of a difference creates expectations, a drive towards communication. Like an arc between oppositely charged poles, the tension produces an effect which removes its cause.

In conversation, then, there *is* difference, but this difference is not felt by participants as particularly significant. Conversation may be thought of as that form of communication where the social, the affective, the pleasurable dimensions, are all in the foreground. This means that participants are treated as relatively equal, and that they have roughly equal rights of participation.

Explanations differ from conversations. They have distinct and unequal roles for participants to fill, namely explainer and explainee. The difference at issue is related to knowledge; the explainer knows something the explainee wants or needs to know. Explainers have a variety of motives *vis-à-vis* explainees. They may amiably fulfil a request for explanation, as when one is asked for directions in the street. They may have a personal duty to explain, as when one has to account for a mistake. It may be their job to explain: teachers and information officers fall into this category.

Thus the difference at issue in explanation is more than simply a difference in knowledge between explainer and explainee. The other crucial difference is in their relationships of power and responsibility. And of course these relationships are complementary.

Everyday explanations generally start from a request for information; the explainee takes the initiative. In teaching, the roles are very different. The context of school sets up the student as needing knowledge – and knowledge determined not by the student but by the system of schooling. Thus one essential difference is that between what the student knows and what the student 'ought' to know. It is assumed that the teacher can bridge this difference. But there is then a second difference: that between what the student ought to know and what the student wants to know. So the teacher may need to provoke, stimulate, demand or coax students into wanting it. This task is not left entirely to teachers, of course. Schools and education systems provide a variety of means of encouraging or obliging students to accept what it has been decided that they need – from published curricula and examinations to systems of reward and punishment. But motivating students to 'want what they need' remains crucial.

One more difference needing to be taken into account is that between established scientific knowledge and common everyday knowledge. Scientific knowledge is not just common knowledge writ large; it is often totally different in kind. It sees the world differently, filling it with new entities – from photons to pharmaceuticals – whose nature and meaning have to be learned. Everyday explanations are in terms of familiar entities doing familiar things. Scientific explanations are often in terms of unfamiliar entities doing unfamiliar things, and the student is a stranger in an unknown world. It follows that much explanation in science classrooms is not the explanation of phenomena, but is the explanation of resources the student needs in order to explain phenomena. Instead óf explaining how sound travels, the teacher explains how to think about waves.

This also means that explanations between teacher and student in science are often shaped by what scientific explanations are available. When the teacher explains about sound being a wave or about chemical bonds being electrical in nature, the explanation forms, as it were, the tip of an iceberg. Unseen, underneath and keeping it afloat is a large hidden mass of scientific explanation. The student experiments with dissolving sugar in water; underneath lies all the science of solids and liquids, molecular theory and thermodynamics. It is this, unknown to the student, which gives point to putting sugar in water at different temperatures.

Constructing entities

Everyday explanations generally fill in for someone a history of how things happened, in a world of known protagonists. The fact that the train was delayed due to repairs to the rails explains the phenomenon of my being late. A loose tile in the roof may account for the ceiling being damp. Explanations of this kind select from a cast of known protagonists and fill out a history which renders the thing to be explained obvious, natural, accountable. But very often, a scientific explanation needs to invoke protagonists which are not part of common knowledge. Explaining to someone then requires describing the possible protagonists as well as accounting for what they may have done.

Indeed, the very phenomenon to be explained may not even be evident. We do not feel our muscles contract to make an arm flex; rather it feels that we flex the arm and thereby contract the muscle. Thus, we cannot ask what biochemical processes contract muscles; *we* do! Nor will a phenomenon seem in need of explanation if one has no idea that it could be explained. Most people recognize that metals are shiny, but they do not think of this as explicable; it is part of what makes metals 'metals'. An explanation about electrons which are free to move, so that shininess is connected with the power to conduct electricity cannot be envisaged. Nor might many people think it sensible to ask why salt dissolves in water or wax melts in a flame. That is just what they do.

It follows that much of the work of explaining in science classrooms concerns the resources out of which explanations are later to be constructed. Protagonists have to be described, with what they can do and have done to them, before any story which explains a phenomenon can be told. Before we can explain how batteries light lamps we have to tell about electric currents, voltages and resistances. Before we can explain respiration we have to tell about lungs, blood, oxygen, carbon dioxide and haemoglobin. Before we can explain burning we have to explain about oxygen, bonding between oxygen and other atoms, and energy.

For these reasons, much of the work of explaining in science classrooms looks like describing, labelling or defining. It has to provide the material for explanations. The entities which are to be used in explanations have to be 'talked into existence' for students. This can be tricky, because their reason to exist is in part their coming role in an explanation. The explanation cannot be given before they are present, but their reason to be present is just this unknown explanation.

The variety of scientific entities needing to be brought into existence for students is large. Some are invisible or intangible, for example microbes or waves. Some are patterns, for example the periodic table. Some are abstract, for example a sinusoidal graph. They may be real but newly minted objects (atoms), instruments (an oscilloscope), relations (Ohm's law), classifications (fluid or gas), processes (melting or freezing), special objects of science (pendulum), or formal structures (straight-line graphs). And, of course, they once all had to be brought into existence in science itself.

Why do we call them all 'entities'? One reason is that they are all new chunks of meaning. Just like real objects, abstract or formal ones get meaning from what they can do, what can be done to or with them, and what they are made from. The other reason is that they all enter into scientific and classroom discourse in a similar way, as 'things' with which or about which to think. They are different, but fundamental work of constructing and using them looks much the same.

The distinction 'about which to think' versus 'with which to think' is crucial. Many scientific entities have to become tools for thought, even if to start with they are only things to think about. They have to become entities which are part of explanations, not things which are explained. So the construction of entities is also the construction of future explanations.

Transforming knowledge

Scientific knowledge is not static. Much crucial scientific knowledge around at the time a person reaches (say) forty years old will be newly made since that person left school. Scientific knowledge is continually being transformed so as to be made accessible to graduate students, to undergraduates, to school pupils and to the general public.

At the same time, developments in technology carry knowledge and scientific and technical awareness into society through their artefacts. Computers on almost every desk are one example; electricity in every home is another. Thus, there is a continual flow of knowledge, outside schooling, from this source. This flow, by altering the nature and demands of jobs, generates new needs in the educational system, thus determining new priorities for the transformation of knowledge. Knowledge has thus undergone much transformation before it reaches the school context. But it is also continually being transformed *in* school.

Entities as they exist for students change all the time. Every discussion gives an entity new possibilities and transforms its meaning – sometimes microscopically (I can use it here) and sometimes hugely (I didn't think it was alive!). The pupil's knowledge is constantly being transformed. An explanation does not 'transfer' an idea – it provides material on which to work to make an idea. These transforming processes were evidently at work in the classroom examples we gave previously. A worm was being transformed into a tube; a joint was being transformed into a designed construction.

One way to transform knowledge is to turn it into a narrative. Stories, whether that of the discovery of penicillin or of a personal experience – say finding food having gone bad – can act as effective 'knowledge carriers'. The narrative relations in the story match the conceptual relations to be understood, and make them memorable and easily recoverable.

The use of analogy and metaphor is crucial to the transformation of knowledge in the science classroom. Examples include the eye seen as a camera and the control of the hormone system by the pituitary gland seen as a conductor keeping an orchestra together. And, as Clive Sutton has eloquently pointed out in his *Words, Science and Learning*, large numbers of scientific terms rely on now dormant metaphor – oxygen the maker of acids, hydrogen the maker of water, alkalis the product of ash, lenses the shape of lentils, and so on indefinitely. We start from the view that analogy and metaphor are not an optional extra, not something which merely sugars the pill of literal meaning. We assume that metaphor and analogy are fundamental to language, to what is called literal meaning (and we note that in this sentence the words 'assume', 'metaphor', 'analogy', 'fundamental', 'language' and even 'literal' all have metaphorical roots – the last two from tongues and from writing). All meanings are made from other meanings, in the end being grounded in meaningful action in the world.

Putting meaning into matter

Scientific theories purport to tell us 'how things really are'. Yet, looking around one, the world does not at all appear to be as scientific theories say it is. Energy seems to be lost, not kept the same all the time. Motion does not seem to go on for ever if there is no force. Sound is not obviously wave-like. Air does not seem to have weight. Scientific theories talk about a world behind appearances, and demonstrations try to bring that underlying world to the surface.

Demonstrations in science teaching are designed to show the natural world behaving as theory says it does. But, as every science teacher knows, they easily 'go wrong'. What is concluded when they do? The failure is attributed to some interfering effect which spoilt what 'should have' been seen. In a sense, then, demonstrations cannot go wrong; the theory they exhibit is not put at risk. But a demonstration is still a confrontation of ideas – which may be what we please – with material reality which will not do just whatever we please. There is still some risk. Theories cannot say just anything we want.

We might say that the job of a demonstration is to get students to see things as theory says they are – that demonstrations are about 'seeing-as'.

Sound is to be seen as a wave; electrolysis is to be seen as a flow of charged particles; tissue is to be seen as made of cells. But this is not quite enough. The point of a demonstration is to persuade one that things *are* as they are shown, to shift from 'seeing-as' to 'being-as'. This means that we have to look at demonstrations as imposing meaning on matter. A demonstration has to be carefully crafted so that the fit of how matter is to be thought about and what it does is as close as possible. Thus demonstration apparatus is as loaded with meaning as a traffic sign or a shop window. An air track almost shouts aloud, 'I make things move in a special way'. But, crucially, not any meaning can be imposed. The behaviour of the material world constrains what meaningful ideas we can make up about it. Demonstrations are therefore an extraordinarily interesting site of the tension between what is supposed to be the case and what is the case.

Orchestrating explanations

We have so far described a variety of dimensions along which explanations can be compared. But it would be a capital mistake to suppose that we have been describing different kinds of explanation, identifiable one by one. Rather, any given explanation has all of these aspects all at once, orchestrated in a particular way. Like a song, which brings together vocal line, melody and rhythm all in one whole, so an explanation brings together the various aspects we have been talking about. Consider for example the following brief exchange between a teacher (Susan) and her Year 9 class which has just finished an experiment detecting carbon dioxide in exhaled breath:

Susan: You can prove that the air you breathe out contains carbon dioxide. Obviously therefore more than you breathe in. Anyone like to have a guess how much carbon dioxide we breathe out [ ] in that air? If your air that you breathe out – the gas that you breathe out is a hundred per cent [*writes 100% on whiteboard*] of what you breathe out – anyone guess how much of that hundred per cent is carbon dioxide? [ ] Matthew?

Matthew: Ninety per cent.

Susan: Ninety per cent. Ricky?

Ricky: Seventy per cent.

Susan: Any more advances on seventy? Darren?

Darren: Eighty.

Susan: Eighty. More? Robert?

Robert: Eighty-five.

Susan: Eighty-five. Daniel?

Daniel: Fifty.

Susan: Fifty.

. . .

Susan: You're all absolutely wrong. No way are you right. OK? It might surprise you– [ ] In actual fact you've forgotten one very important thing. There's something in this air outside that we hardly – we don't use at all. We take it in. [*Gestures towards mouth*] We push it out. [*Gestures away*] Don't use it at all. Don't touch it. Don't use it. Don't react with it at all. What gas is that, Daniel?

Daniel: Nitrogen.

Susan: Well done, OK. Nitrogen is in the air out here, around me, OK? And over seventy per cent of the atmosphere around us here is nitrogen. It goes in. [*Gestures towards face*] It goes out. [*Gestures towards face*] It doesn't play any role at all. It might surprise you to know that only [*pause, writes on whiteboard*] four per cent of the air that we breathe out is carbon dioxide. That's a very small amount. That indicator is a pretty good indicator.

First, difference. By getting guesses which are wrong the teacher creates a difference of view; there is reason to explain. Second, constructing entities. At least two entities are under construction, 'respiration' and 'the atmosphere'. Third, transformation. The natural process of breathing is being transformed into a biochemical affair of exchange of gases. Fourth, demonstration. Susan's gestures evoke an actual physical process of movement of gases.

There are, of course, many ways in which explanations can be orchestrated, and many aspects of difference, construction of entities and transformation which may be at issue. Thus we have to think about some of the sources of their variety and about some of the ways in which they can be put together. One source of variety is the context of surrounding explanations. Explanations hardly ever appear as isolated single events. They nest inside and fit alongside one another, to form larger patterns which are themselves explanations. Explaining the periodic table, or the behaviour of waves, may occupy many lessons. We cannot understand why what is being explained at a given moment is being explained unless we look at this larger picture. Similarly, many lessons have an overall explanation plan – often clear only to the teacher – into which smaller acts of explaining intelligibly fit.

Another source of variety is the teacher. How a given teacher explains has a personal history – a history of experience and of relationships with pupils in the class. We cannot understand how a given teacher is explaining something without having some idea of what resources of authority, knowledge, experience, materials, etc. this teacher commands. Only rarely does one see an explanation newly minted in the classroom. Mostly, teachers bring out well-practised forms; 'good' explanations are part of their stock in trade. Teachers are also careful to stimulate just those interactions with the class which they feel confident of managing with that class in that context.

Variety also arises from what is going on at that moment in interaction with students. The question a student asks may call for an explanation. The answer a student gives may need to be elaborated or corrected. Ideas which might be used to construct an explanation may need to be collected from the class. At other times, a way may have to be found to gain attention for a lengthy or complicated explanation. Previously given explanations may need to be recalled and restated. And so on. All these kinds of interaction, some not foreseeable before they arise, will influence how explaining is done, and what kind of explaining is required. Which of them arise will depend on what kinds of interaction the teacher allows or encourages.

The subject matter in hand also has a pervasive effect on choices of what and how to explain. Scientific ideas vary in kind and difficulty, so choices are continually being made of what to explain, what to assume and what to avoid. These decisions depend on the nature of the entities concerned: Are they visible or invisible? Are they natural or artificial? Are they objects or processes? Are they concrete or abstract?

Teachers put all these things together in a variety of styles. One such style is that of the 'teller of tales', of explanations given or knowledge 'carried' in the form of stories. The classical stories of scientific discovery – Newton and the apple, Kekulé and his dream, Wöhler and the accidental synthesis of urea, Fleming and the chance discovery of penicillin – are part of teachers' stock resources and carry explanations about how science works. Some physical processes such as infection by a disease, the movement of continents or the making of steel, can readily be put in narrative form.

A very different style is that in which the teacher arrives at explanations through collecting and reshaping ideas from the class. We may call this 'let's think it through together'. It requires continual to and fro between opening up opportunities for contributions and reworking and 'making official' ideas which have been obtained.

A style we may call 'say it my way' has a focus on explanations as ways of talking. Explanatory forms of words are laid out and practised ('If the frequency increases, the pitch [?]'). Explanations are often implied in the grammatical roles which terms are permitted to play – for example in 'Its energy makes it go further', 'energy' is treated as an active causal agent.

Many scientific explanations require one to see things in a certain way. The space round a magnet has to be seen, for example, not as empty but as filled with an unseen magnetic field. The teacher using the style 'see it my way' sets out to try to get students to see phenomena, such as iron filings round magnets, waves sent down springs, or water evaporating, as they 'should' be seen from the point of view of a certain theory. 'Rough edges' in what is seen are ignored or excused; reality is presented as exemplifying the theory. Demonstrations may try to show how after all the theory does 'get it right'.

The structure of the book

This first chapter has attempted to give an overall view of the arguments and evidence to be found in the book. The rest of the book elaborates and justifies them, and shows how they work out in practice.

Chapters 2, 3 and 4 open up and analyse our three main groups of categories for analysing and comparing explanations. Chapter 2 deals with creating differences, with motivating explanations in a variety of ways. Chapter 3 discusses the construction of entities, both concrete and abstract, object-like and process-like. Chapter 4 describes a number of kinds of transformation of knowledge, both in adapting it to school science and in transforming it as students learn. Chapter 5, starting from the role of demonstrations in explanation, shows how in science meanings and material things have to be brought together.

Chapters 6 and 7 begin the synthesis as – having taken explanation apart – we try to put it together again. Chapter 6 traces sources of variety in explanation, and Chapter 7 looks at a number of styles of explanation the teacher may use.

Finally, Chapter 8 draws together the main ideas and points to issues, questions and problems which the work here has brought to light.

Chapter 2

OPENING UP DIFFERENCES

A difference of opinion

Let us start with the obvious. When people differ in their understandings, there is a need for them to explain their ideas to one another – unless, of course, they 'agree to differ'. In the extract which follows, the teacher (Leon) provokes a disagreement of this kind on purpose. All the students in his Year 9 class are girls.

Leon: Do you think that you can tell if you're having a baby or a, or, if you're having a boy or girl, by, where, the where? [*gestures a rounded belly*]
Student 1: The shape of it, that's what I heard.
Student 2: I don't believe that.
Student 3: That's what I heard.
Leon: Who from?
Student 1: From you. [*The teacher is stunned*]
Student 3: My auntie.
Leon: Oh, your auntie, must be true. It must be true.
Student 4: [*To another student*] Don't laugh about it.
Student 5: It's funny. [ ]
Leon: So are you trying to tell me – okay, think of this little, this little foetus, about to be born right, okay, has it gone through secondary sexual development?
Student: No.
Students: No.

Leon: Okay, a little baby brother, a penis about this big, okay. [*Teacher holds fingers close together in front of his eyes*] [*Student laughter*] True? True? You're telling me, that that alters, the swelling [*Teacher makes a curved shape with his arms around his stomach*]

Student: But you can tell if you're having a boy, like because your bump gets bigger, and if you're having a girl it's normal.

Leon: Oh.

[*Students laugh*]

Leon: I would like to s–, I would like to see the paper in *Nature*, that established the – that data, yeah. Do you think its likely, Aisha, that a penis on a little baby boy, is going to affect a pregnant mother's bump, in any way? Do you think it's likely? I'm not saying it's true or false.

Student: It might.

Leon: You think it might?

Students: Yeah.

Student: It depends upon if the woman's having a girl or boy.

Leon: Pardon?

Student 1: Because, if she's having a girl, she gets uglier and fatter, and if it's a boy

Student 2: No, no she doesn't.

Student 1: That's what I've heard.

Student 3: I heard this sir.

Student 4: I heard different.

Student 1: If, if it's a girl

Leon: Uh-uh.

Student: [*inaudible*]

Leon: Yeah?

Student 1: if it's a girl

Leon: Yeah?

Student 1: it becomes round.

The differences here look like differences between persons and what they believe or entertain to be the case. The persons are unequal in status: the teacher feels free to appeal to scientific authority. He produces an argument against the belief (the argument that a penis makes no appreciable difference to the size of a foetus). The students range against that argument 'what I have heard' or 'what I have been told', and they do not give up. After all, they know perfectly reputable adult people who hold and use this belief. Thus the difference becomes, not that between what Leon believes and what one student believes – a matter of a difference of opinion between two people – but a matter of a difference between cultures; between home and school, between the everyday and 'science'. The argument turns from being about what teacher and student happen to believe to being about what students 'ought to believe'.

We thus see that the difference behind the surface which motivates the discussion is a difference between what students know or believe at the moment and what they might know or believe in the future. It is directed at changing their understandings. The teacher has decided the direction of that change – this is after all an event in school. So the difference is at bottom between what students think now and what someone has decided they *should* think. Nevertheless, what keeps this classroom interaction alive, and produces its unusually high level of dispute and spontaneous intervention by students, is the strong sense which is still there, of a difference between two people. They do not agree, so they had better talk.

What drives explanation?

We often speak of 'resolving our differences'. We speak of 'tension' or 'opposition' between points of view, and of situations as creating such tension and explanations as relieving it. A nearby metaphor is that of friction – of different ideas grating on one another, creating a need to explain and to 'smooth' the movement of thought. The underlying image is one of conflict and force as driving communication.

The other main metaphor is of 'distance apart' and of 'moving from one position to another'. We speak of 'being stuck', of a 'blockage' to understanding, of being 'unable to follow', or 'unable to see'. When we understand, we can 'get there', 'see it', or 'follow it'. Explanations become paths across gaps. A related metaphor is of possession: 'now I have it'. An understanding, once elsewhere, is now in my grasp.

The reason for this small excursion into metaphors is twofold: to suggest ways of looking at what a teacher has to do in order to create a need for explanation, and to link our work here with that of those who analyse discourse more generally. Some theorists interested in communication and discourse, who want to account for what makes people communicate, use the metaphor of 'difference', as we indicated in Chapter 1. The metaphor is close to but more generalized than the idea of 'distance' mentioned above. Often, 'difference' is understood as a *difference between two people*. It may be a difference of knowledge, of power, of interest.

Certainly in the science classroom there are differences between people, especially between teacher and student. And these include all three kinds of difference: of knowledge, power and interest. Teachers and students know different things, are able to do different things, and are concerned to achieve different things. This is the fundamental backdrop. But, and it is a big but, in the science classroom there is another player – the physical world needing to be understood. Science teachers frequently offer to join students in the attempt to understand it, often signalling that shift with the use of 'we'.

Teacher: If we were to imagine that that is the case, OK?, it would presumably have a magnetic field around it.

Teacher: If we took a big piece of carbon and we cut it and cut it and we had a very special microscope and a fairy scalpel – and we cut and cut and cut and cut – then eventually we would end up with millions and millions of these separate little bits of carbon, and they would be called atoms. And if we cut them any more, then they wouldn't be carbon any more.

What this kind of use of 'we' does is to blur the distinction between the human participants, and to encourage a focus on what is being talked about. Of course, the use of 'we' is a symptom, not a cause. It arises when the teacher has done work to create a social situation of acting together to learn, of joint agency. This is done in many ways, small and large. One small one is completing a thought together:

Teacher: Microbes, and you need a micro [?]
Students: scope [*Teacher says it too*]
Teacher: to see them.

A much larger one is the example with which we began this chapter, of teacher and students arguing together. Another is the teacher 'thinking aloud', with hesitations, false starts and re-attempts. This may be an attempt to explain, or – more involving still – it may be creating something for students to think about, as below:

Leon: . . . then what – what do you see? What do you actually see? . . . is that what – remember when we saw – I drew the one with three beams of light coming in – what happened to that? Did it go out? Did it – did it actually refract outwards? Did it? Because – look – we said – we said that this part – this part at this end was just like a bit of a prism, OK? So if light came in – if light came into that part – imagine that's a prism there, right?, where does it refract to?

The hesitations, rephrasings and repetitions here are not, in our opinion, 'lack of clarity'. They signal that here we have 'thinking in progress', and so that there is something really to be thought about. By contrast, a question like, 'What happens when a light ray strikes a lens here?', signals something very different: 'what you ought to know', and locates the difference back between teacher and student, not between the student and the phenomenon to be understood.

We want to say, then, that explanations in the science classroom are mainly driven by differences between what students know now and what they need to know. For this reason teachers often talk in the tense of 'We are going to . . .': the future in the present. Part of the job of the teacher is to open up, to create, this difference. Of course, merely being in school tells the student that some such difference will be at issue – one is supposed to be there to learn. But – and in science this creates a lot of work for the teacher – it is often not easy for the student to see in advance just what difference in understanding needs to be bridged.

Creating interest

Let us return to the obvious. Students are 'naturally' interested in some things, and when they are the number and variety of questions they ask increases notably. Common areas of interest include environmental issues and – even more so – bodily functions, especially sexual, as in the example below from Year 10. The teacher is David.

Student: What's that?
David: It's underneath its tail, this is a male rat, and that's its
Student: What happens when you're constipated, what causes that?
David: Wait on, wait on, let's have one question at a time. Just sit down and wait. Right, as I was saying
Student: Is that his willy?
David: That is its penis.
[*Laughter*]
David: We might as well use the correct words.
[*Laughter*]
David: Here are its testes.
Katie: Can you get female rats?
. . .
Student: Don't be such an idiot, Katie. How do they do reproduce?

Science teachers face the task of creating interest in many other matters of much less concern to students. Perhaps the movement of continents is not too hard a case, once students have been told the surprising fact that they do in fact move. How to electrolyse copper sulphate or measure the acidity of a solution is less obviously fascinating, though both may be linked to their practical uses in hope of making them more appealing. The question of what determines the period of oscillation of a pendulum, not to mention how to analyse motion under gravity, might stand as prototypes of the supremely uninteresting, whilst acknowledging their passionate interest for physicists.

One obvious way of sustaining interest is through story-telling. We have more to say about this in Chapters 4 and 7. For the moment, let us note an example from a lesson concerning the extraordinary events surrounding a French-Canadian fur trapper Alexis St. Martin whose stomach was opened by a gunshot wound, and whose doctor used the opportunity to study the process of digestion:

David: . . . suddenly the doctor thought, 'Wait a minute, this means I could look through that hole and see what's happening to the food while it's being digested.'
Student: Oh, and he could see.
David: That's right, so he said to this bloke, he said, 'Look, why don't – why don't you just stay here for a few days and – you know – just have free breakfasts now and again, and I'll just have a look thr– look through this hole, and see what happened to your

breakfast as you're eating it?' So they did this, and the doctor wrote these great long diaries of what was happening, he took bits of – he took bits of boiled egg, for example, and tied the bit of boiled egg onto a bit of string, stuck it through the hole, and then he st– took the time, 'Eight o'clock', 'ni–', you know, 'nine o'clock', stuck a boiled egg through [*mimes waiting*] 'five past nine', pulled it out, had a look, to see what was happening, wrote down what was happening, stuck it back in. And he did this for day after day after day, with all sorts of different foods, sticking it through the hole, pulling it out, looking to see what was going on . . . Anyway, that's how they discovered what was happening inside the stomach.

The whole bizarre story can be found in Chapter 7. Beyond its immediate (and perhaps dubious) appeal, the story serves other interests. Its force comes in part from the special collision between eating as everyday experience ('have free breakfasts now and again') and the biological interest in digestion as a biochemical process ('I'll just have a look . . . and see what happened'). The continued oscillation between the two worlds of personal well-being and of 'scientific observation' is striking, and gives the tale its ghoulish character. It offers a definite – and not wholly sympathetic – image of the kinds of interest science has in things. We will begin Chapter 3 with a similar example, but there seen from the point of view of transforming the objects of concern – of seeing them differently.

This example leads us to broaden the notion of 'interest' somewhat, beyond 'natural curiosity' or 'entertainment'. Teachers cannot, and in our data do not, try to make everything attention grabbing. This is simply because much of what is of interest to the sciences is not of immediate fascination to students and cannot be made so without deforming it. What is a matter of interest, of concern, what is a problem, varies from one culture to another. The cultures with which we are concerned are those of the everyday (in our case Western industrial) world, and of science – and specifically science in school. Quite generally, but very importantly in this particular case, cultures decide what it is important to attend to. Culture decides what counts as problematic. 'Interest' now becomes, not what one finds appealing, but one's main concerns; what one is trying to achieve (as in the sense of the phrase 'an interested party'). And the problem is that the sciences have their very special interests which are not necessarily shared with others. Understanding the motion of things like pendulums is one of them, for reasons not to do with pendulums but to do with much larger issues, namely understanding the causes of motion throughout the universe. The teacher's task is to reproduce some such structure of interests in students, if possible. That is what it would mean to make them 'more scientific'; it would be to make them ask the kinds of question central to the interests of the sciences. And this is no small matter: to change one's interests is to become a different kind of person who belongs in a different culture.

Much of the remainder of the chapter concerns how teachers set about creating new structures of interest – interest in our wider social sense – in scientific explanations.

'What we're going to do next'

Science teachers frequently need to explain the nature of a new topic, before anything much of the new topic has been understood. There is a simple but crucial difficulty in doing so: brief statements of the meanings of the new ideas to be learned are more or less incomprehensible. We illustrate this with an example from a Year 6 textbook, taken from a discussion of definitions in Halliday and Martin's *Writing Science*:

> A circle is a plane curve with the special property that every point on it is at the same distance from a particular point called the **centre**. This distance is called the **radius** of the circle. The **diameter** of the circle is twice the radius. The length of the circle is called its **circumference**.
> (quoted in Halliday and Martin 1993: 72)

If one did not know what a circle was this would not be the way to find out. And if one does, it may look even more peculiar. The text is not telling you what a circle is. It is showing you how, in geometry, mathematicians think about circles. And it is all too plain that the mathematical culture has a very unusual kind of interest in circles. This interest interlocks with others, including plane curves (whatever they may be, from the student's perspective), and terms like 'radius', 'diameter' and 'circumference'. Even in this elementary case there is a lot to understand before one can understand anything. Each element gets its meaning from the others. It is this interlocking of meanings which makes it hard to get started simply with a set of new ideas. We give another example in Chapter 3, concerning the meaning of 'density'.

On the surface, the next example shows the teacher (Elaine) co-opting Year 11 students' interest by starting from ideas and associations which they already have. We will see however that in fact she has a much deeper concern than doing simply that.

> *Elaine*: Right. What we're going to start on today is a new topic, and it's called 'organic chemistry'. So can you put that as your main heading please?

Elaine is well aware of the lack of meaning to students of such a heading, and that difficulty shows in the responses to her next questions.

> *Elaine*: Anyone have? – got any ideas what this topic might include? From the word organic? Yes?
> *Student*: . . . growing things.
> *Elaine*: Growing things. Okay. Don't write this down. Let's just put up some of the ideas that you've got. Growing things. Can you be a bit more explicit about that?
> *Student*: Health . . . growing . . .

Elaine: Sorry. Health. Natural. Okay. Healthy. Put some hands up – the
       word organic – what does it mean?
Student: [*Inaudible*]
Elaine: Sorry? Crops

. . .

Elaine: Sorry – somebody said? Shampoo. Right.
[*Murmurs of surprise and amusement*]
Elaine: Fine. Any other ways you've met this word organic?
Student: Food.
Elaine: Food. Right.

As this interaction continues, Elaine can bring out that the main associations of the word 'organic' are with living things. She does so because she
is going to spring a surprise. The surprise is that 'organic chemistry' is not
the chemistry of living things, but is just the chemistry of carbon compounds, and that this includes the chemistry of living things, but much else
besides including such non-natural substances as plastics. So this introduction, easily mistaken for a case of 'eliciting what students know', is going to
be used to undermine what they know. The 'organic', the 'natural', are to
become not what they seemed. And Elaine will do this through telling the
story of the accidental synthesis of urea – an 'organic' substance made from
inorganic materials at a time when this was thought impossible because
'organic' substances were held to need some special contribution from living
organisms:

> *Elaine*: . . . they thought that these special chemicals could only be made
>   inside living things or they were the waste products of living
>   things or the decayed products of living things. In fact, they
>   had a theory called the Vital Force Theory.

More of this episode can be found in Chapter 4. Here our concern with it
is the way it confronts the clash of meanings and the differences in interest
between science and everyday life. To do organic chemistry is to ask a completely new set of questions; no longer questions like, 'Is this substance good
for you?', but questions like, 'How many carbon atoms do the molecules of
this substance contain?'. Elaine's job has been both to expose this difference,
and through interaction with the class and some history of chemistry, to try
to bridge it. The work she is doing opens up two complementary differences:
firstly that between the student now and the student later, after learning
organic chemistry, and secondly, that between the interests of and questions
proper to two different kinds of knowledge about living materials – the
scientific and the everyday.

Utility

A common strategy in introducing a new topic is to stress its usefulness. Indeed Elaine, in her introduction to organic chemistry just discussed,
deploys this strategy too:

Elaine: Now, do you want the good news, or the bad news?
Student: The bad.
Elaine: The bad news – there are about, and I could be out of date on this by now – but the last time I was reading about organic chemistry – there are about three and a half million different carbon compounds.

. . .

Elaine: Carbon forms about seven or eight times as many compounds as all the other elements put together. It's an extremely important part of chemistry because it's the chemistry that we use when we're talking about biology, the chemistry of carbohydrates and proteins and things like that. It's also the chemistry for producing the things that we take for granted now like plastics, dyestuffs, the things that 100 years or so ago, weren't around. And we just take them for granted now, all our synthetic fibres, for our clothes, our nylons, terylene, our polystyrene ceiling tiles, our polyurethane foams for furniture and so on. Right, now that was the bad news, but the good news . . . is we don't have to learn about all of them and those that we do have to learn about can be put into groups. Within a group they have quite a lot in common so you really only have to learn about one member of the group, then you can make some pretty good guesses about all the other members of the group. So we can organize our knowledge about these different carbon compounds into discrete little packages which is going to make it much easier for us to learn.

Elaine evokes three kinds of 'usefulness'. They are utility (i) for understanding biology, (ii) for making new and useful materials and (iii) of organization of knowledge to make it easier to learn. Thus she appeals to students' expected 'natural' interests in living things and in technical novelty, but also to their concerns as learners. Or, to put it differently, she creates three kinds of difference between students as they are now and as they might become: a change in knowledge of things that already interest them, a change in what they are interested in towards the interests proper to chemistry, and a change in the facility of their job as students. Correspondingly, the 'we' in this passage shifts from being 'we as ordinary interested people' to 'we as chemists' and then to 'we as students and teacher together'.

One might perhaps see all this, taken together with the part of the introduction discussed earlier, as close to motivational overkill. It certainly seems as if Elaine is trying to make it as difficult as possible for students to reject what is to come, by appealing to as many facets as possible. But what she is also doing, in quite a short space of time, is establishing several kinds of difference which will be at issue: differences to do with what chemistry is like, with what knowledge is available from it, and with the business of learning it.

There are, of course, many examples of simpler and briefer appeals to utility. For instance, in David's lesson on digestion:

David: . . . but I've forgotten to tell you about hiccoughs, and you all want to know how you get hiccoughs don't you?

Promises and anticipations

A good many science lessons start by naming the topic to come, and this may include some kind of definition of what it is about. We are interested in the function of such a step, so far as later explanations are concerned, over and above having a heading written in students' exercise books. Here is the start of one Year 10 lesson:

Tom: OK, the alkali metals. [ ] So what – would you start off by doing [ ] is copying those first three into your book. Copy the three boxes into your book. It may be bigger.
Student: Sodium.
Tom: Lithium, sodium, potassium.

The teacher is going to do a demonstration (see Chapter 5 for an extended account of this lesson) to show the similarities and differences between the three elements, the nature of which leads to their being called 'alkali metals'. This and other such groupings of elements will be crucial to much later learning of chemistry; indeed it is very common to use this group of elements to introduce the very idea of such groups. One might argue that it would be better if the label 'alkali metals' were to come at the end, when some reason for choosing it had been provided. As it is, it is no less 'incomprehensible' than the circle was previously. The name comes before the basis for the name.

This argument, however, is to mistake the function of this kind of action of a teacher. The title is best understood as making a promise. It names something not yet known and promises that it can and will be understood. A difference is opened up between where students are now and where they will be, in the shape of a blank but labelled conceptual space. Interestingly, the form of the lesson to come actually implicitly follows this metaphor, 'filling the space' item by item with a comparative table of the properties of the three elements. Providing for that exercise is indeed the reason for the initial activity of copying boxes to be filled in.

Near the beginning of Chapter 3 we give an example in which a definition (of 'density') also functions as a promise of understanding to come – an interesting case since definitions are usually envisaged (wrongly in our view) as clarifications, not as things identifying the 'not yet understood'. The definition of a circle, discussed above, must function in the same kind of way.

Here are some further examples of talk near the start of explanatory episodes which are also, in the above sense, not yet strictly comprehensible, but which serve to promise an understanding, and so once again open up a difference between students' present and anticipated knowledge:

Teacher: . . . electricity and magnetism are two things which are very closely related, OK?

Teacher: ... you will see how a computer can be used in an experiment, and it is going to make a graph. I also hope by the end of the lesson you will understand better how graphs work ... I've got two things here which can make scientific measurements.

Teacher: I'm going to summarize the periodic table for you ... we're going to look at drawing particles in relation to the periodic table.

Teacher: Now, a pendulum is basically a very simple thing. All there is in a pendulum is a piece of string and something hanging on the end which swings.

The first may be quite mysterious to someone who knows nothing of electromagnetism. The second will only make much sense when one finds out what it is to use a computer in an experiment, or what 'how graphs work' could mean. The third promises the 'drawing of particles', but what could that be, 'in relation to the periodic table'? And the last tells you what a pendulum is without hinting at why it should be in any way interesting or deserve so solemn a baptismal name.

In no way do we want to suggest that the teacher is making any sort of 'mistake' in producing such statements. It is a quite common strategy, though teachers may not be aware of it as a strategy. And it is not necessarily a problem for students. They learn to understand such utterances as a harbingers of work to come which will make the utterances make sense.

What do you expect?

Teachers constantly draw on students' expectations, as another main way of creating a difference which can produce a need to explain. We use the term 'expectations' in a broad sense, ranging from letting students see surprising phenomena to getting them to commit themselves to an answer before finding out if it is right. First we illustrate these two, and then fill in some others.

Counterexpectation

The example with which we began this chapter, of a discussion about whether pregnant women could tell the baby's sex from the shape of the 'bump', is a case of confronting one set of expectations or beliefs about phenomena with another. It clearly creates a tension to be resolved, or a gap to be bridged with further understanding. Even if the teacher's biological rejection of the idea is accepted, the issue still remains as to why reasonable people known to and trusted by the students believe it. A large and important difference is created; that between two worlds of knowing and their respective authority and basis.

In the next example, it is a student who draws attention to a counter-intuitive phenomenon. The teacher, Alan, has asked who knows anything about the eye. Here is what is salient for one Year 8 student:

Student: When you [ ] the pictures in your eye [ ] it doesn't come straight
away like the right way round – it – it comes upside down.
Alan: Good. Good. So the image that's formed in our eye might actually be upside down.

The issue is not forgotten. At the end of the lesson Alan returns to it:

Alan: The image gets picked up by the light-sensitive cells in the retina,
and messages are sent to the brain, and it's actually the brain that
effectively turns that image the right way round so that we see
things the right way up.

If this addresses the difference created by puzzling about how upside-down
gets to be experienced as right-way up, it does so only partially. It opens up
yet further queries, notably how a brain could possibly do such a thing. And
that this is so is signalled by the use of 'effectively', indicating that there are
mysterious depths here which it is not now proposed to plumb.

Chapter 1 contains another example of counterexpectation, when a teacher
shows a class that they have all grossly overestimate the amount of carbon
dioxide in exhaled breath.

'I wonder if I'm right?'

Although science teachers often ask questions and nominate or allow one
student to answer – often to the relief of those passed over – they sometimes
get a whole class to commit themselves to an answer, so raising the tension
at least a little. Early in a lesson on joints in the skeleton the teacher (Leon)
gave out statements to judge true or false. He insists on a clear answer:

Leon: 'Bone is not a living tissue.' Is that true or false? I don't want you
doing one of those 't's where you can change it into an 'f'.

Soon he and the Year 10 class come to the answers to this question:

Leon: Next question?
Student: Bone is not a living tissue.
Leon: True or false, bone is not a living tissue. False, it's most
definitely,
Student: It's the first question I got right.
[*Student laughter*]
Leon: It's a living tissue. Why do some people think of bone as not
living? It's a psychological thing.
. . .
Leon: I, well what I believe about this is, whenever do you actually
see it?
Student: You don't.
Student: Cut yourself.
Leon: No, when do you actually normally see bone?
Student 5: When you

Student 1: When you
Student 5: cut yourself.
Student 5: Yep, or when you bring out that skeleton obviously.
[*Student laughter*]
Leon: Okay, let's get one thing, when you actually see the skeleton is that bone living?
Student: No.
Student: No.
Leon: You see, so what some people think about bone, is based on, what you s–, you know, you see skeletons, and you think of them like, some sort of like mineral compounds, stuff, yeah, just looks like, like
Student: Because they're in the ground.
Leon: so, you think of it, like, dead stuff. But bone, is very much alive, yeah? Because what can you actually take from some people [?] and put them into other people [?]
Student: Bone marrow.
Students: Bone marrow.
Student: Bone.
Leon: Bone, you can do bone grafts can't you? So it mu–, it's living stuff, it's actually living, and it grows, it's living, totally, it's not like a dead bit of your body, it's absolutely alive.

The existence of an issue – a difference to resolve – is very clear in these lively exchanges. The bringing into existence of that issue must owe something to the prior commitment of each student to an answer. The students had formed some expectation of what the answer might be, and were interested in how it would turn out. A difference was created and helped drive explanations of why bone is living material and of why one might think the opposite. This device, of getting all students to commit to a position before discussing an issue, is a way of distributing difference amongst everyone. It is probably underused in science lessons – certainly we saw it quite rarely.

We turn now to a variety of other examples in which students' expectations are either used or challenged, making space to be filled with new meanings or creating tensions to be resolved.

'Imagine that!'

Meaning-tension can be created by seeing or thinking about surprising or unusual things. A sign that this has happened is that students themselves start posing spontaneous questions. They sense the difference that has been created. Consider the following example of a difference created but not much used, in a Year 8 lesson about the eye:

Alan: Has anybody ever cut an eye up and had a look inside?
Students: Ugh!
Student: Can we do that?
Alan: Not this year, I'm afraid – no.

The work in fact then turns to looking at pictures of the construction of the eye. There is no doubt that the idea of dissecting an eye produces feelings of revulsion in many people. As in previous examples, a difference – indeed a gulf – opens up between the human feeling for our eyes and our sight as precious possessions, and the objectifying mode of biological investigation of their structure. This difference is here neither used nor explored, fertile though that might have been. But evidence that the tension remains is provided by a number of questions students raise later in the same lesson, after Alan mentions the matter again:

Alan: ... if at some stage in the future you see a demonstration of an eye being cut open
Students: Ugh!
Alan: and actually take the lens out, and you can have a look at this lens [ ] you'll see
[*much chatter*]
Alan: You will see
Student: What year will we do that in, sir?
Alan: You might do it in GCSE.
. . .
Student: When you've taken the eye out, does the pupil still work?
Alan: It won't respond then – the eye will effectively be dead.
. . .
Student: Is it true that if you push there at your eye you can take your eye out?
Student: Oh don't!
Alan: I very much doubt it. I wouldn't try.

Has this to do with expectations, as opposed to just being 'natural' feelings of revulsion? We think so. It has to do with the meaning of our eyes to us, and so with how we expect to feel when dissecting them, contrasted with how we are being expected to feel – the latter signalled by the objectifying language used by the teacher. The gulf between the two worlds is, however, not always so great in this lesson. At another point, Alan is talking about the action of the pupil of the eye:

Alan: So if it is quite dim – if there isn't very much light around – then your pupils have to open to allow as much light in as possible. What might happen if it was very very bright and our pupils were wide open?
Student: They'd get small again.
Student: They'd get damaged.
Alan: You could possibly damage your eyes ... there'd possibly be too much light for them to respond to – so the pupil closes down again to limit the amount of light.
Student: How can you? – If your eyes are open and it gets? – How can it control it?
Alan: Oh you don't do it consciously. It all happens for you.

Student: You still get damaged though you can't do anything about it if your eyes are wide open.

. . .

Alan: But what would happen is your eyes would automatically respond. For a brief moment they might be too wide, but they would automatically respond. You don't have to think about it. The pupil starts to close up straight away, OK.

Student: When you're in bed and the light just comes on – when your mum comes in –

Student: Yeah.

Alan: OK, yeah – brilliant example of it . . . So you've woken up in the morning – you're lying there in a darkened room and you're struggling to see something. Your eyes – there's so little light around that your eyes really have to struggle to make out any shadows or anything like that – so your pupils are wide open to get as much of that light in as possible – and . . . somebody walks in – switches on the light – and you go 'uh!' – like that [*covers his eyes*] – you've got to cover your eyes up. And it takes just a very short period of time for your eyes to readjust, doesn't it?

Here what students know and expect is not being challenged, but is being used. And these are not just 'examples' to illustrate what they know. They come from the students' own thinking. Thus one student wants to know what controls the pupils; how such a thing happens without being willed. Another quite spontaneously offers a good example (being woken up and the light turned on). All this suggests that the students really are thinking about what to expect to happen.

Problems to think about can often involve making sense of potentially surprising facts. In a lesson about sound, Alan uses a textbook question about whether two astronauts could talk to one another in space:

Alan: . . . there are two astronauts on those pictures. They've called one of the astronauts Neila and they've called the other astronaut Glen. Now then, Question 2 is saying, why couldn't Neila hear Glen even if he was shouting? This is the first picture. You can see Glen go, 'Whaa!'. Neila can't hear a word, yes?

Student: Is it that there's no air in space?

. . .

Student: What they're wearing is stopping it from getting through, isn't it?

Alan: Is it? Is it? We'll have a look at that in a moment. If we have a look at Question 3, they say that when the helmets touched, what did Neila's voice have to travel through to reach Glen? So the assumption there is that when the helmets touched they could hear each other – Neila could hear Glen. So what did the sound have to travel through?

. . .

Student: The glass in the helmets.

We must notice here that the (Year 8) students are not accounting theoretically for what they know to happen, but are asked to work out what 'must' happen from what they know theoretically. Theory is driving 'fact'. What one should expect is the driving idea, and what happens is going to be made to fit. The reason, of course, is that the lesson is about the theory, not about the phenomena. A later passage in which theoretical results are 'inferred' from fantasy facts helps make it clear that this is what is going on:

> *Alan*: Well the fact that if they had some new radios they could hear each other – so what would that prove to us that radio waves can do? . . . OK – so the radio waves that are going between their radios must be able to travel through space.

There are thus two different kinds of 'imagining strange things'. One is seeing something strange and not easily explicable, such as an upside-down image, a ball supported on a jet of air, a big spark from a small battery – and so on. The phenomenon is unexpected and the issue is one of explaining it. The other is hearing one of the stranger explanatory stories of science, such as motion going on for ever, light travelling through nothing, or the unfolding of a new organism from a single egg. Now the problem is one of coming to terms with the odd behaviour of the entities in that story, and of believing that the phenomena it suggests actually happen (can astronauts not hear through space? does the stretching of time in relativity really happen?).

'What do we think now?'

We must avoid giving the impression that creating differences, motivating explanation, is something to be done at the beginning of some explanatory episode – to get things going – and to be abandoned afterwards, as the now-wanted explanation unfurls. On the contrary, it happens continuously. As bits of explaining get done, students have to think what each means, and whether there are gaps yet to be bridged or tensions to be resolved. 'Does that mean that if . . . ?' questions from students are one sign of such work going on. Below, a Year 9 student checks with the teacher (Tom) if a newly created way of thinking about measuring volumes makes sense.

> *Tom*: So if I wanted to know what your, what your volume was, you'd get a big dustbin, and you'd get in it, and you'd get under the water for a second and you'd see how much water overflows.
> *Student 1*: You might get killed trying to get out.
> *Tom*: Well you have to do it very carefully, under strict controls.
> *Student 2*: Sir, erm, say, you've got a massive swimming pool, like say about thirty people, and you've got, say, twenty people going in it, you'd put one by one and then you'd measure
> *Tom*: measure how much it grows, that's right, that's it.

Sometimes students who want to test out an idea, or who find difficulties with their understandings, will speak up, but the extent to which this happens varies widely from class to class and teacher to teacher. From the considerable number of such questions which can on occasion arise, we believe that only a small proportion of such cases find overt expression. Clearly, in classrooms where turn-taking is tightly controlled, the proportion will tend to be low.

It is not necessary, however, for the teacher always to place responsibility on students for bringing out difficulties or ideas. One possibility is to tour the class looking at work being done and asking questions, and then 'publishing' the problems discovered to the class as a whole. The following excerpt shows the results of such a classroom 'tour' by the teacher of Year 7 students working in groups at a number of tables:

> *Steve*:   Now, mmm, I've been trying to find out and I've spoken to most of the tables, about what's happened in this experiment and I'm going to ask certain people now what's happened. I'm going to say people's names. I don't want people shouting out, and at the moment you don't need to put your hand up, because I'm just going to pick people by names to say what's happened. Daniel, what's happened in the experiment?
>
> *Daniel*:   Arr, mmm, the wax melted into water.
>
> *Steve*:   It melted into water? So, Daniel, have you got, in your tube at the moment, have you got some wak–, have you got some water?
>
> *Daniel*:   Yes, sir.

Daniel would probably never have asked, 'Is water the right name for this watery stuff?' Nor would the other students in the class who probably had the same thought. So Steve asked a question in full knowledge of what the answer was going to be, having heard Daniel's ideas previously.

Where Tom's student had an idea and checked it out, Steve's had an idea which Steve discovered and Steve ensured that it was checked out.

'Nothing to explain?'

We conclude with an example of a very difficult case of creating differences; of disturbing how to think and what to expect. It is the case of making what seems obvious into something not obviously to be expected, but which needs explaining. In what follows, Leon sets himself the problem of making the simple and obvious fact that we see things 'where they really are' into something to be explained in terms of the way light travels. It cannot be easy, if only because in everyday thinking, we reason the other way round, that things are where they are because we see them there.

> *Leon*:   I'd agree with you that the stars are the furthest sources of light that we can see – right? – they've travelled a long way. Right? And it comes all the way through space – yes? – all the way through space . . . in straight lines to us. So if we see a star and it looks in the sky as though it's there [*points*], right? – in that

line – over there – where really is it? If it looks to be over there [*points*], is it really down there [*points*]?

Student: No.

Leon: Has the light gone, sort of like, from over there, 'nee-ee-um' [*gesture and sound of rapid motion in a curve*] something like that?

Student: No.

Leon: What's the light done? It's just gone 'zy-oom' [*gesture and sound of rapid motion in a straight line*] straight to us, yeah? It travels in straight lines, right? Do you see what I mean? If I wanted to smack you across the head, right? – I don't – I don't – I never would want to do that – but if I wanted to do that, right? Or give you this pen. If I wanted to give you this pen, yes? Would I – would I put it into your hand 'cos really your hand's there? Where really is your hand?

Student: There

Leon: Yeah. And I know that, don't I? How do I know your hand is in that line from me to you?

Student: 'cos you can see it.

Leon: But how can I see it? What? – there's light in the room, there's light coming in, and where is it shining?

Student: Everywhere.

Leon: Is some of the light shining here? [*points to student's hand*]

Student: Yes.

Leon: And then what does it do? Shines on to you?

Student: And reflects.

Leon: It reflects. To me? Does it reflect to me in curved lines or in straight lines?

Student: No, straight lines.

Leon: So it's coming through [*gesture towards teacher*] – so if I want to put this pen in your hand I can go straight along the line that the light's coming from, and put it in your hand – right – and that's in your hand isn't it?

We see Leon here tackling one of the most fundamental problems of explaining scientific explanations, that is, dealing with cases where there seems to be absolutely nothing to explain. Indeed what is about to be explained is that which, in everyday thinking, itself *does the explaining*. Leon has not only to make it seem a problem that he can see a hand where it is, but has to get further involved in making it a problem that he can see the hand at all. Instead of a story of light travelling from hand to eye, common sense has a story of light 'everywhere' which is a condition of seeing but not a mechanism of seeing. People do the seeing – the presence of light helps. Notice the response, 'Everywhere' to the question, 'Where is it shining?' (from Year 8).

A limiting, but fundamentally important case of dealing with expectations is thus that case where there are no expectations at all – the case of the seemingly obvious. There are more than a few such in science. Things fall when we let them go and stop when supported by the ground. It is obvious and we use it to explain events, not as an event to be explained. What need of 'gravity' here? Take another: animals move around by themselves. It is hard to persuade anyone that there is something to explain here – how they do it and why. 'Motion by itself' is part of the meaning of being 'animate', telling us what is animate and what is not. It explains; it is not to be explained.

Here is Leon again, in a different case, trying to make something 'obvious' into something to be explained:

> Leon: . . . how do plants know in the autumn to drop their leaves? How
> do they know? What, how would they know, as it were, to know,
> to grow towards the light? Yeah, I mean, there must be some sort
> of chemicals, yeah? – influencing what happens with them.

Two main kinds of difference

The many ways of creating difference discussed in this chapter can perhaps usefully be grouped into two main kinds. One kind is when the difference is between what students do not know and what they need to know. These are grouped under the heading 'What we are going to do next'. The other is when the difference is between what students think they know and knowledge which runs counter to that. These are mainly grouped under the heading 'What do you expect?'

Chapter 3

THE CONSTRUCTION
OF ENTITIES

New things from old

A teacher, David, is talking about teeth:

> *David*: Your teeth are part of your digestive system, your teeth take the
> food, smash it up into tiny bits, bite it off, smash it, make it into
> tiny bits.

What is going on here? Several accounts are possible: David is explaining
the function of the teeth; he is explaining a part of the process of digestion;
he is developing 'the concept of the digestive system'. But what strikes us
most about it is that the teacher is trying to change what 'teeth' are for the
students. The students already know a lot about teeth, from early childhood
and beyond. They know about what they can do and what can be done to
them, about where they are and what they are. They have been constantly
reminded to clean them. They may remember losing milk teeth. They have
experienced dental care. They know – not necessarily consciously – that
teeth are important in smiling. They have been prevented from biting other
people. But now the teacher wants them to imagine teeth differently, not
now as a part of the mouth, and not now in relation to feelings, but as a
component of a biological system. Words like 'chew' associated with inten-
tional action are avoided; instead the teeth are presented like machinery
('smash it up into tiny bits'). So our account is that the teacher is busy
constructing a new entity, the entity 'teeth in the digestive system'. Teeth are
being given new meaning, just as (say) 'banks' are given new meaning when

considered by an economist as part of the invisible economy, instead of as a place in the High Street where one gets money.

Here from the same Year 10 lesson is more of the digestive system 'under construction':

David: So before we start, what bits do you know you've got in your digestive system. Tell me the names of some of the bits you've got.

Student: The small intestine.

David: The small intestine. Where do you think that is?

Student: Down here.

David: Down here somewhere.

Student: No.

Student: Here.

David: It's about here. In fact, it's called the 'small intestine', goodness knows why it's called the 'small' intestine, cause it's really big. The small intestine are about here, okay, or maybe they're about here, but anyway, what else what else have we got?

Student: The large intestine.

David: You've got a large intestine. The small intestine sits here, where does the large intestine go?

Student: On top.

David: That's right, good. It goes across the top, then around, and comes back, and actually finishes up at the, at the anus. What else have you got? Katie, what've you got?

Katie: The bladder.

David: You've got a bladder. It's not part of your digestive system. That is part of your excretory system, that takes waste out of your body.

David is changing the students' understanding of the digestive system. He is also changing their understanding of various parts of human bodies, the large intestine, the small intestine, and the bladder. On the surface, these changes seem simply to be a matter of telling them things. But not just telling. Notice the intense focus on things here and now ('Where do you think that is?' 'Down here.' 'Down here somewhere...' 'No.' 'Here.'). A lot of gesturing and pointing is going on. The students are being asked to stand outside themselves as persons and to regard themselves as objects in the world. The objects – the entities – which make up their world are being changed and added to, including their own bodies.

There is a reason to change their world, a reason which derives from the nature of explanation. The everyday explanation of eating is that food is nice as well as necessary, sociable as well as personally satisfying. It satisfies wants. The biological explanation tells a story in a different world, made of organs, juices and biochemical processes. The biological actors in the story of digestion are not at all the social human actors of the everyday business of having lunch. So to get to the biological explanations, the resources needed – the relevant biological entities – have to be constructed. And constructing them means establishing what they can do, what can be done to them, and what they are made of. We showed in Chapter 1 how this way of looking at what is involved in meaning derives from combining a Piagetian viewpoint with a semiotic one.

In Chapter 1 we also briefly discussed the nature of explanations and the special nature of scientific explanations. We presented scientific explanations as analogous to stories of how things come about, but with the actors in the story often being unfamiliar and new. Here we see a small example of the introduction of new actors. These particular new actors – these new entities – are not especially new to students, however. That is one good reason for the teacher wanting to make teeth seem strange, so as to suggest that there *is* something new about them to consider. Later in this chapter we will see much less familiar – much stranger – entities under construction, including some that it would at first sight not seem reasonable to think of as 'entities' at all.

Here is one further extract from the same lesson on digestion. The class are looking with the teacher at a dissected rat.

Student: What's that black stuff?
David: That bit there is the liver.
Student: It looks like it's been smoking.
David: That bit there is the stomach, Katie, that bit there is the stomach.
Students: [*Light laughter*]
David: Okay, and now what she's looking at, is this stuff here, which is the liver. People don't realise how big the liver is, livers are really big. That great chunk there is liver. So when she says it looks like it's been smoking, she's thinking that this is in fact lungs. If you were to look at the lungs of somebody who's been smoking, they're not pink and soft like they should be, they're black and gritty, and that's why, that's why you said that . . . nicotine and tar . . . Anyway, that's the liver. Now, the liver, is a place where food is stored. The liver's part of the digestive system, I guess, because eventually food is taken from the – from the gut, via the blood, to the liver, and stored in the liver till need it's needed, okay?, so, for example, if you have for lunch four Mars bars and you . . . four Mars bars – then the stuff would go to the, to your gut, all the sugar in those Mars bars, which would be a lot, would come straight back to your gut, and into your blood, and your blood would be like treacle, because it'd be full of sugar, so in fact, it's taken straight to the liver, and it's stored in the liver, and small amounts are let out, uh, through the course of time, okay?, so that's the, that's a kind of storehouse where things are stored, so the liver stores food, it does a whole load of other jobs, but it stores food.

This seems like the naming of parts. But it quickly develops into an explanation of what the liver does, a story about digestive events. Starting from a student asking, 'What's that?', we get a story about sugar and livers, not just a naming. And there is good reason for this: what the liver *is*, what it can do and what can be done to it. So the explanation, giving the liver a role in an explanation, is indeed part of the job of constructing the biological entity – the liver. This new entity is smoothly linked to several other things: to the perceptual knowledge the children have gained by looking at it, and to knowledge of livers and foods which the students already possess. The way the explanation is given, with its choice of a familiar context, tells the students that the new knowledge about the entity is meant to add to, not to replace, what they already know. And the easy – indeed unmentioned – assumption that rats' livers do the same job as human livers says implicitly that we are talking about livers in general, not about livers in rats.

We have made a case that much of the work to do with explanation involves students and teachers together constructing new or modified entities – entities which will become resources for making explanations. Some explanations have the function, not primarily of explaining a phenomenon (though they may also do that), but of illustrating what role a new entity may play in other explanations, which is part of constructing new meanings from what things can do and have done to them. The students have work to do, but that work is not always discovering knowledge already in themselves or in the world to hand – though it may be that too. Their work is also to make their own sense of explanations and of resources for explanation offered by the teacher.

Making a new conceptual entity

The teacher in the extract below, Tom, has the perhaps unenviable task of introducing his relatively low ability and sometimes difficult Year 9 class to 'the concept of density'.

> *Tom*:   Right, listen, what we want to do now is have a chat about, mmm, what this word means, density.
>
> *Student*: I know.
>
> *Tom*:   Now, I'm going to tell you what density means, and then we're going to go and have a look at how you can measure it.
>
> *Student*: Is it the same as on a disk?
>
> *Tom*:   No, well, in a way, what, you mean like a computer disk?
>
> *Student*: Yeah.
>
> *Tom*:   How much information you've got? In a way it is.

As in previous examples, these students are encountering something new. As yet, 'density' is just a word to them, but the teacher effectively promises that it will become something more. For the term to develop, the teacher will have to perform a lot of work, over a long period of time, and the students will have to be active participants in that work.

One student is already seeing if he can create his own tentative understanding, employing his understanding of the term in another field. Other students are likely to be doing the same even though they merely seem to listen. The way this student thinks ('the same as on a disk') points to another vital aspect of the construction of entities: building them by analogy with others. Interestingly, the term 'density' as used in the label, 'Double-sided high density', on a computer disk derives from an analogy of information density with material density – from an analogy with the very scientific term 'density' which the teacher is here involved in constructing. The student, more familiar with computer disks than with ratios of mass to volume, does the same job backwards. We return to the role of analogy and metaphor in Chapter 4.

Even at this early stage, it is not hard to see that something new is coming into existence, a new thing which may still seem to be a 'term', a 'word'. And the teacher talks in a way which has an air of 'explaining terms': talking about 'meaning', defining terms and giving examples, as below:

> *Tom*: Density is how much stuff there is inside a thing. Now, to give you an example of what I mean by that, Michael, that's made of wood, okay, this piece is made of metal, which one do you think is heavier?

Rather quickly, however, the teacher moves from words into *activities* which seem quite different. In fact, he stops talking about density and puts pieces of wood and metal before the class, discussing which is heavier and which is bigger, and he *does* things together with the students, having them weigh various objects, and having them *look* at the objects to make guesses of their size. The work is directed at *things*, not at a *word* any more. The teacher dared to assume, with a 'lower ability' class, that the students would understand that he was talking about 'density', when he was actually talking about 'weight' and 'wood' and 'metal'. And the assumption held. The students can 'read' this kind of classroom work.

The teacher does not refer to density again until some time later. When he does, he uses a new term, 'mass', and he places a qualification on the things in question. They are now not just things, but *things which are the same size*.

> *Tom*: That one would sink. This one is denser than this one, so two things the same size, one has got more mass in it than the other one.

What is striking here is that what the teacher is saying cannot yet make sense to the student. The experience is very familiar. New definitions generally seem distinctly opaque (if the reader is not persuaded we advise looking at some definitions of 'money' in an economics textbook!). Of itself that is not necessarily a problem; at various points in their school life students will encounter similar and no less mystifying 'definitions', which will later – and only gradually – come to make sense. In this lesson the teacher moves quickly to give the definition a more permanent form, and makes the students write it down:

Tom: So, . . . the first thing we're going to do is write down what density is. So copy this down.

[*The teacher writes on the whiteboard*]

Student 1: Density is

Tom: Density [ ]

Student 2: Density

Tom: We'll just call it stuff for the time being, it doesn't matter [ ]. Density is a measure of how much stuff there is in an object.

No matter that this was Newton's definition of mass, not of density. Much later in the lesson, after practical activities measuring the volumes and masses of a variety of objects, the definition of density is transformed again:

Tom: Yeah. So you know what you measure, mass is measured in grams, volume in cm cubed, okay. So, if you wanted to know the density of something, what you'd be interested in is how many grams of stuff are there in every cm cubed of space that you've got.

Over the span of a whole lesson, 'density' is gradually constructed. Here are the successive transformations:

• how much stuff there is inside a thing
• two things the same size, one has got more mass in it than the other one
• a measure of how much stuff there is in an object
• how many grams of stuff are there in every cm cubed

The entities of the teacher's talk gradually 'come into existence', are constructed. And the teacher does not assume that the job is now done. The last form of 'density' is rehearsed through repeating a meaning and a form of words in several successive examples:

Tom: Let's have a look and see if you know what to do. Meesha, what do you think is, has got more grams for every centimetre cubed, the piece of lead or a piece of wood?

Student: Piece of lead.

Tom: Piece of lead okay, Tim, what do you think has got more grams for every centimetre cubed, a piece of glass or a piece of polystyrene?

Student: Piece of glass.

Tom: Well done, so it must be, you want to try another one, right, what do you think has got more grams per centimetre cubed then? No, no, sit down, I'm asking a question. What's got more grams for every centimetre cubed? A piece of wood or some balsa?

Student: Wood.

Tom: Right.

The repetition 'says' several things: that these are all parallel cases; that the new idea is to be used in the same way in each; that it *is* the same idea in each. It repeats one of the things one can do with the entity 'density', namely deciding which of two things is more massive. And the form of words ties an expression to what the class have just been doing with their hands when measuring the masses and volumes of different objects.

By having the students write down the definition the teacher indicates that density will be recurrently important in their work in science. But terms such as 'density', or 'stuff', do not make sense simply *because of the definitions*. The teacher may *say* what density is, but the students do not, as a result of that saying, *know* what density is. To say what density is, isn't *to mean*, but is effectively to make a *promise* that the utterance will be meaningful in retrospect. Students can recognize that these utterances have a particular status; from the slow pace of speech, a particular intonation, their repetition, and the fact that they are often to be written down and remembered.

'Density' will continue to be transformed. Over several years it will be implicated in a wide variety of relations with other entities – floating ships, 'floating' continents, gases, mercury and barometers, the atmosphere and the weather, convection, and even in ways of distinguishing chemical elements. It will participate as an entity in a multitude of explanations. In all this, as it becomes related to other things, it will be undergoing yet further change. The students will be learning more of what you can do with this entity. For example, in Tom's lesson, density cannot be a property of a gas, since, for the students, gases do not yet clearly have any mass. When eventually the density of a gas is considered, both 'gas' and 'density' will be changing into something else, each a little different. Density will now apply to seemingly intangible things. And a gas will as a result come to seem more tangible, more substantial. Thus, in these later incarnations, the entity 'density' may not obviously be changing, but change there will be. 'Density', like other entities, does not come into existence and remain what it is for all time. Meanings of entities undergo constant change, though where the change is less dramatic it may be barely noticeable.

Why 'entities'?

We referred above to the teeth and the liver as 'entities'. In the discussion of density in the section which followed, we have referred to 'density' variously as a term, a word, a concept, an idea; but we have also, and with less obvious justification, called it an 'entity', as if it were to be thought about in the same way as the teeth or the liver. Why insist on it as an 'entity', implying that it is constructed in the same way as others? There are several reasons.

First, we do not find it helpful to distinguish 'explanations of material things' from 'explanations of concepts'. Certainly verbal forms of definition play a role in the latter which is not so obvious in the former. But the discussion of material things in the classroom involves a lot of definition. For example (coming from Year 10):

Leon: There are two parts to a human skeleton, two sections. Well, not really. Not like you can go, shlip, and there's one part and there's one part, but we classify it as though there are two parts. Did anybody learn those two parts, that there are to the human skeleton . . . They are, write it down, axial, A X I A L, A X I A L, and in brackets you want to say what's in the axial skeleton.

Student: What's in it?

Leon: Umm, skull, spinal column, skull, I said column at the end,

Student: Skull, spinal column.

Leon: and ribs [*teacher touches his ribs*] Yeah? Because after all, what's, like, the axis of something? The main stem, the main part, right. The next part of it, of the skeleton, will be, appendicular. A double P [ ] E N D [ ] I C U [ ] L A R. Appendicular.

Student: Um, like appendix.

Leon: Appendix, on the end, yeah, like stuck onto it. Now, what's stuck onto the skull spinal column and ribs [*said very quickly*], what's stuck on?

Second, the distinction between the material and the conceptual is not at all clear-cut in science itself. A magnetic field is both a real thing and a concept. In Chapter 6 we give an example of a teacher turning this concept ('the locus of directions of a compass needle') into a tangible entity with its own proper actions. A chemical bond or a wave are similarly conceptual and real at the same time. Forces and accelerations are concepts, but are also talked about as things which affect one another.

The third reason is fundamental. By thinking of all the elements that enter into scientific explanations as 'entities' of some kind, we can give a uniform account of explanations. We can think of explanations as being like stories in which actors play out their roles, and we can think of the actors (the entities) as the things which the student has to learn about. An explanation of (say) motion as produced by gravity fits the same form as one about insulin controlling sugar levels in the blood.

A fourth, and again fundamental, reason has to do with how meanings are created and made. As we understand them, meanings are constellations of possibilities; they are what something can do, can have done to it and what it can be made from or make. Such a formulation covers 'nouns' and 'verbs' as well as 'planets', 'acceleration' as well as 'electricity', 'density' as well as 'livers'. Of course *what* can be done with 'density' is not the same kind of thing as what can be done with 'livers'. But learning their meaning is in many ways the same kind of job.

In this perspective, connections can be made between the material activities Tom provides (handling blocks of many different materials and attending to their look and feel) and the talk about the 'concept' density. Tom provides materials which are commonly used to make objects, but he does not use them to make objects. The materials are to be seen in a new way. They are presented in a special way, as bland regular blocks without the individual features which would give them identity or suggest a function –

that is, they are presented as 'substance' rather than 'object'. Where a steel spoon would have said, 'use me', the teacher's regular steel blocks in the context of the lesson say 'measure me'. The material objects are being transformed too, into things which are measurable in three dimensions, that have volume and mass, for which the relation between 'the space they fill up' and their massiveness is salient and important. Thus materials get new possibilities and new meanings. And all this looks forward in the curriculum to a time when materials like these are to be seen, not as stuff with which to make things, but as stuff made of something – of atoms and molecules.

These kinds of transformations are common and fundamental to science. Eating becomes digestion; falling becomes the effect of gravity; our stable home, the Earth, becomes a rocky ball hurtling through space; what parents pass to children becomes DNA; feeling unwell becomes an affair of microbes; plugging in the electric kettle becomes a current flowing under a potential difference; and so on. It is not enough to say that these transformations just involve knowing a bit more. They change the inhabitants of the world.

We take up this theme of transformation again in Chapter 4. To think about how entities are constructed *is* to think about how they are transformed. Everything new is made from something old. Some entities made in the learning of science are radically new, but there is much seemingly mundane construction work to do as well, as here in Year 9:

Tom: Right, as Katie correctly says – sorry, Donna – Donna correctly says [*teacher holds up an object to the class*] that is a, all together now [?]
Student: a plastic tube.
Tom: Measuring cylinder, it's not a plastic tube. Right, it's a measuring cylinder, okay.

However, to see a plastic tube as a measuring cylinder is to do more than learn the name of a tool. To understand the entity 'measuring cylinder' is also to understand more about a different kind of entity, 'volume'. And there are not two distinct activities, 'learning the concept volume' and 'recognizing measuring cylinders', there is just one, with 'measuring cylinder' and 'volume' coming into existence together. The measuring cylinder is significant because of its relationship to the concept 'volume', and the concept 'volume' may in large part develop through the use of measuring cylinders. Their features – their markings for measurement, and their three-dimensionality, help 'carry' and concretize the notion 'volume'. We can see something of this complex joint construction process going on in the following, with the same class:

Tom: Right, now let's decide. Volume is now – [ ] Yes right – [*the teacher raises the measuring cylinder in front of the class*] it's the amount of space something takes up, the volume is like the amount of space something takes up [*teacher starts pointing to the measuring cylinder*] so if I build it up to 100, Kathleen, that means that that is holding a 100 centimetre cubed worth of space, or worth of water, yes?

Resources for explanations

David's story about digesting a chocolate bar is clearly an explanation. It tells how something comes about. Much of the explanatory work of the science classroom is devoted, however, not just to explaining phenomena, but to constructing the entities with which explanations of phenomena may be built. Whereas the working scientist may well be concerned to find an explanation for a particular phenomenon, say, the depth of soil to which rainwater penetrates, the work of the science classroom is directed at future potential classes of explanation, at for example how things move or flow, or at how atoms bond together.

The point of teaching, and explaining, is thus not simply to explain a particular phenomenon which may be immediately in question, but is to create a *resource* which may be used to explain a whole variety of phenomena, often by creating resources on which later schooling will depend. Considered in this way, a very wide range of classroom activities are to be seen as involving explanation.

To illustrate this we borrow an example from Jay Lemke's book, *Talking Science*. The teacher asks what element is being represented by a particular electronic configuration of electrons in an atom.

Teacher: If I have one electron in the $2p_x$, one electron in the $2p_y$, [ ] two electrons in the $2s$, two electrons in the $1s$, what element is being represented by this configuration? [ ] Ron?

Ron: Boron?

Teacher: That would be – That'd have uh [ ] seven electrons. So you'd have to have one here, one here, one here, one here, one here [ ] one here –

Student: Carbon.

Teacher: Who said it? you? What's [?]

Students: Carbon! Carbon!

Teacher: Carbon. Carbon. Here [*points to periodic table*]. Six electrons. And they can be anywhere within those – confining – orbitals. This is also from the notes from before.

(Lemke 1990: 240–1)

Several explanatory resources, with large and important future potential, are here under construction. There is the entity, the periodic table – a display of chemical elements patterned simultaneously by chemical properties and the numbers of particles their atoms contain. There are the entities referred to (mysteriously to the outsider to this game) as $2p_x$ or $1s$ (which are forms of arrangement of electrons). There are elements – boron and carbon. And of course there are electrons.

We note particularly the focus here on *things and what they do*. But 'what they do' is not something which plays a part as yet in explaining a phenomenon – as it might be if it were electrons carrying an electric current or making light on a television screen. Here, 'what they do' is about 'how they are'.

This particularly complex set of interrelated entities is valuable for its future potential. They will make it possible to explain such things as the differences and similarities between chemical elements, why some are metals and others are not, why some react easily and others do not, why water has two hydrogen atoms for every oxygen one. Whilst a description of all of these entities could perhaps be got into a chapter in a book, a compilation of explanations of all the phenomena which they can be used to generate could fill a library and still not be exhausted.

The example is extreme. A simpler case is the following, in which Steve is teaching a Year 7 group about melting:

Steve: Shamir?
Shamir: It's liquid.
Steve: Right. Okay, it's a liquid, like water, it's a liquid like water. Can you just explain what you mean by that.
Shamir: It's like, umm, it's runny.
Steve: It's runny. You can pour it [*teacher picks up test-tube*] you could pour it out of the tube. It's a liquid.

'Liquid' is much more than the 'correct scientific term' for runny things, though that may be how it seems at that moment. 'Liquid', along with 'solid' and 'gas' will gradually be transformed into 'states of matter'. And the reason to do that is not at all a matter of terminology. It is that different kinds of explanation are appropriate for accounting for these different states, and also that these different states play very different roles in creating explanations of other phenomena, whether the strength of bridge girders, the way to get a balloon to rise, or under what pressure oil has to be pumped down a pipeline. Thus the 'terms' solid, liquid and gas are pointers to different kinds of explanation. They help organize knowledge about differences and overlaps between explanations.

Our conception of 'entities' as resources for making explanations embraces a very wide variety of things, an 'ontological zoo'. A few examples might be: water, energy, animals, fluids, density, amplitude, convection, evaporation, newton-metres, mass, volume, electrons, electron shells, line graphs, equations, variables, friction, cubic centimetres. Even this small sample points to the enormous amount of work which is required to build 'worlds' in which these things make sense and can be used. The list does not distinguish material and abstract things. Distinct though they are at one level, for us they are all 'entities' at a more abstract level, because of the uniform way they enter into explanations.

Providing resources to be used later obviously has its problems. It may seem to students too much like a case of 'medicine today, jam tomorrow'. For this reason, teachers need to provide effective motives for attempts to construct entities. These can be of many kinds, from appealing to the exigencies of the syllabus to involving the students in thinking out how things might be. A good example of the latter appears in Chapter 7, where a teacher gets a class to think through with him what joints in the skeleton might be

like. Some teachers are able to work with students so that entities are co-
constructed by teacher and class together.

There are other ways of providing motives. The 'entity-coming-to-exist'
can be put to use in some partial explanation of something real, preferably
familiar. David was doing just that on the process of digesting something
sugary. In the example below, the teacher is building up the entity 'hormones', but makes time for a number of particular examples of the working
of hormones, in this case by questioning the class about what happens when
you get a fright, having been asked about it by a Year 9 student:

Leon:	Umm, okay, umm, so, umm, that's another gland called the adrenal gland, A D R E N A L. Adrenal gland [*writes 'adrenal gland' on the whiteboard*]
Student:	That's what makes adrenalin?
Leon:	Yes, well done, Myra. Ad-re-nal gland and it produces adrenalin, yeah.
Student:	Is this for girls *and* boys?
Leon:	Yeah, well, well everybody does this one, yeah. Yeah, the boys get frightened just the same as girls.
Student:	Ohhh.
Leon:	What's it for? [ ] Why would you want, your lungs, why would you want your rib cage to sort of come up to about here, and your diaphragm to go down to about there and then come back again? What are you trying to get a lot of?
Students:	Air.
Leon:	Well particularly [?]
Students:	Oxygen.
Leon:	Oxygen, yeah, and your heart instead of just going [*makes small gestures over his chest*] toom, toom, toom, goes [*makes very large gestures across his body*] fe-toom, fe-toom. What are you trying to get round your body?
Student:	Blood.
Leon:	Lots of blood, which contains [?]
Students:	Oxygen.
Leon:	Oxygen, and [?]
Student:	Food.
Leon:	Food, right? What does that sound, like you're trying to get ready to do?
Student:	Spree. [*Student laughter*]
Leon:	It sounds as though you're trying to get ready to do [?] Nasma, it sounds as though, you're trying to get, you're going to get ready for something pretty active, yeah?

As always, not one but many constructions are going on at the same time,
many of them in students' minds. The girl who asks, 'Is this for girls and
boys?', does so in the context of the whole lesson, which has touched earlier on sex-related hormones. A possible shift in the meaning of gender is in
the air: 'boys get frightened just the same as girls'.

In all these examples, the teacher's talk is crucial, as an example of how to talk, indeed of how to think. The very point of constructing entities as resources is that they need to become, not things to think *about*, but things to think *with*. This is the importance of teachers demonstrating in their own talk a process of thinking which will allow the formulating of questions and of answers to questions, that is, demonstrating how to think with and manipulate one's knowledge.

And not only that. It is also part of constructing entities as thinking resources for students to try using them as such. Having worked with a Year 8 class on light rays (another entity at once abstract and material) Leon's next teaching step is to challenge the students to put them to use:

Leon: I want you to draw something that looks like this.
Student: A wiggly line.
Leon: No, like this. Glass rod. Okay, that's just a glass rod, a bit of a glass rod. Draw this please all of you.
Student: Pardon.
Leon: Draw this. It's a bit of the glass rod, and the question is, how can light, which travels in straight lines, OK, light travels like that, straight lines, how can it, erm, get to the end? [ ] How can it possibly do it?

The answer to such a question is an explanation, a possible story about the behaviour of certain entities (here light and glass), and the way in which this story accounts for how an event might come about. We don't reproduce a student's answer above, because there wasn't one. Leon knew that this process – making up an explanation – would take time; and he made time and space for it. For a substantial fraction of the lesson, students worked on the problem and Leon moved amongst them addressing problems they raised about it.

Process entities

Scientific texts are well known for their high concentration of events and processes presented as if they were things. Simple examples include evaporation, crystallization, ionization, speciation, oscillation. Any scientific textbook or journal will yield a multitude of them, as transparent as 'magnification' or as opaque as 'commensurability oscillations in the resistivity' (culled from a relatively non-specialized journal). Their presence is not due to the barbarous linguistic habits of scientists. They exist in texts and talk as entities because they exist in the thinking of scientists as entities. They are, as we said before, things with which to think.

Our next example shows a teacher (Steve) working on constructing a process with Year 7:

Steve: I want to finish off the lesson by just making sure you understand the word 'melted'. If you get a teaspoon of sugar and put it in a cup of tea, it, it does not melt. [ ] It goes into the liquid, and you can't, you, don't have little bits at the bottom anymore but it has not melted. If you get an ice-lolly and you hold it in your hand for half an hour, it will melt. If something changes from a solid to a liquid, it melts. If you have a solid which disappears when you mix it, and this is very important, what, if you've got a solid which disappears when you mix it with a liquid, that's is not melting, there's another word to describe that. Esther, what word do you use to describe what happens to sugar in tea?

Esther: It dissolves.

Steve: It dissolves. So make sure you understand the difference between dissolve and melt. They're not the same as each other.

We argued above that although one would not initially consider a process such as 'melting' to be an entity, it is an important characteristic of science that it carefully examines such processes, and in examining them does turn them into something like things. In smelting iron and in studying glaciers we see 'the melt' discussed, for example. We have earlier made the point that the entities which interest science are hardly just 'material things', and here we find yet more 'objects of study' for science which are, in this other way hardly material objects, entities such as 'digestion', 'hydrolysis', 'meiosis', 'convection', 'radiation', 'excretion', etc.

Entities and their parts

So far we have mainly looked at the construction of meaning for entities in terms of what they can do and what can be done to them. A further aspect of making meaning for entities remains to be examined. It is 'what they are made of': the parts they have, and the other entities of which they are parts. Entities come as complex packages: a cup has a hollow space, a rim, a base and a handle. These features contribute to the meaning of a cup. The lungs have parts such as air passages and blood vessels, and are themselves part of both a physical thing, the body, and part of a conceptual entity, the respiratory system. All these facets contribute to the meaning packaged up in the entity 'lungs'.

In some cases, the parts of entities are straightforward physical subcomponents. We have seen two examples above (parts of the digestive system and parts of the skeleton). A further example is the following (Year 8) account of part of the eye, the retina:

Alan: . . . if you look at the retina there are two main types of cells in the retina OK? Cells in the retina respond to light, so if you shine light on them they respond, OK, they do things [ ] and in fact what they do is when light shines on them they send – they respond by sending messages to your brain, and it's your brain that does all the hard work . . . In your retina there are actually two different types of cells – two main different types of cells. One of the cells responds to coloured light, OK? The other cells respond more to black and white light. OK? When it's dark in the evening at night times and so on, can you see colours? Or do you tend to see in shades of black, white and grey?

Student: Black, white and grey.

Student: You can see green.

Alan: You see green?

Student: If they're bright.

Alan: You certainly don't see the variety of colours that you see during the day – OK? – most of you have probably noticed that you see things in black, white, shades of grey in between . . . that is because one of the types of cells in your retina . . . responds more to black, white and grey than to colour. And it needs less light to do so.

In introducing parts, Alan focuses – as in many previous examples – on what they can do and what can be done to them. The role which the parts can play in an explanation, here of night vision, is an essential part of their meaning. One expects an organ like the eye to have parts, but some entities have parts much less obviously. Here is Leon stressing to Year 8 that lack of obviousness in the case of light itself being made of colours:

Leon: Have you, did you ever have one of those Barbie dolls? Yeah? Okay. Right, excuse me, if you, if you, take this leg off, and this leg off, and this arm off, excuse me, this arm off and the head off, right? You've got all the parts, yes?

Student: Yes.

Leon: Stop . . . the Barbie doll, you took the bits off, yes, and it's just like parts now. What happens if you, put this leg on and this leg on and this arm on and this arm and it's head on?

. . .

Leon: It's a Barbie doll. So if you've got white light, yes, and you can separate it into all its colours – red, orange, yellow, green and blue and violet – what happens if you put red, orange, yellow, green and blue and violet back together again?

Students: They're white.

Leon: OK, right, that's how it works. I didn't think you'd get that one 'cause it's a hard one, okay.

Leon enforces the not so obvious idea that white light can be 'taken apart' into colours and then 'put together again' by the analogy with a doll which can obviously be taken apart and put together again. The analogy is not one which says anything about what light *is*. It is one which says something about what can be done to it.

Just as entities, in our way of thinking, are not at all restricted to physical entities but can be conceptual, so parts can also be conceptual. Chapter 7 contains a lesson on sound, which can be read as introducing the conceptual parts 'amplitude', 'wavelength' and 'frequency'. A conception is being imposed and laid over the thing – sound – itself, and in that process the entity 'sound' is transformed. Similarly, in Chapter 6 we give the example of magnetic fields being constructed as 'made of' lines of force, and emphasize there the work that goes into making these abstract parts of an abstract entity seem real.

Amongst other important kinds of entity with parts are crucial tabular and diagrammatic knowledge structures such as the periodic table or the carbon cycle. Below we can see the teacher (Year 9) explaining the parts of the carbon cycle as she builds up a diagram:

Elaine: [*Points to diagram*] . . . I started at the top – carbon dioxide in the atmosphere. Draw a box – it might be better to do the writing first and draw a box around it . . . Right – carbon dioxide in the atmosphere – and that stays more or less the same amount all the time because some things put carbon dioxide into the air and other things take carbon dioxide out of the air.

Student: Trees cut down – and if they're not cut down.

Elaine: That's right. Two reasons for not burning down the rainforest, isn't it?

. . .

Elaine: Right, now how does the carbon dioxide get into the air?

Student: We breathe it out.

Elaine: OK, so that's – that box says 'animals breathe out carbon dioxide during respiration'. Respiration . . . again, I would write it first if you know how big a box, but remember that you've got to get a box over here, and a box over here, and a box in the middle, so keep it within those sort of limits.

The emphasis on the existence of parts to be filled in ('a box over here') and on the physical act of drawing the diagram, may serve to enforce the idea that this entity – the carbon cycle – is a structured whole. But there is emphasis also on the structuring principle; that the parts consist of classes of entities taking part in classes of processes which give rise to flows of carbon dioxide *into* or *out of* the atmosphere. It would be very reasonable of the students to expect there to be arrows added from or to the 'carbon dioxide box'. Once again the nature of the parts is explained by what they do or what is done to them.

Prototypical explanations

Particular explanations use particular entities to account for a given phenomenon. But learning science is just as much learning about *kinds of* explanation, which differ in detail but are similar in form. For example, stability in biological organisms is accounted for in terms of controlled checks and balances between the actions of various influences. This scheme is used to explain the control of body temperature, of hormone levels, and even of the rate of breathing. It may be termed a 'prototypical explanation'. In this way an entity which fills a certain role (e.g. control) in one such explanation, for example a hormone, becomes more than a hormone. It is also a regulator – a general class of entities (see Chapter 4 for an example of an analogy with an orchestra and its conductor, clearly intended to lift the argument to this more general level). And, of course, a hormone is already a class of entities, including progesterone and testosterone as members.

An example of a lesson about a prototypical explanation and the classes of entities it involves is one on weathering. The interchanges between the teacher – Elaine – and the Year 7 students continually shift level, from particular cases to what they are cases of, and back again.

Elaine: So, what is weathering? What do we mean by weathering? Yvonne?

Yvonne: Weather can wear it away.

Elaine: Right – not necessarily wear it away but [?]

Student: Damage it.

Elaine: Damage it and loosen it, so that perhaps the surface looks crumbly. Right, so that's damage, to the surface of rocks or buildings, stone, brought about by things like wind and rain and frost – the different weather conditions – which is why it's called weathering. Pollutants. Scientists think that pollutants might speed up this change, might make it go faster. What do we mean by a pollutant?

. . .

Student: Something in the atmosphere.

Elaine: Something that pollutes the atmosphere. What do we mean by 'pollutes the atmosphere'?

Student: Changes that makes it bad, like put bad fumes into the air or something.

. . .

Elaine: Changes the air in a way that causes some kind of problem or damage. And how does that pollution get there?

The prototypical term 'weathering' is exemplified ('things like wind and rain and frost'). The general term 'damage' is illustrated ('perhaps the surface looks crumbly'), after being substituted for the slightly less general idea, 'wears things away'. In this lesson, this talk is leading up to an experimental activity in which students will see whether different concentrations of dilute acid affect different materials at different rates. Its point is that Elaine wants the students to see the activity, not as testing the effect of acid on some materials, but as a prototypical explanation of pollutant concentrations altering rates of weathering.

Much of schooling in science necessarily concerns such prototypical explanations and classes of entities. Teaching about electric circuits is not teaching about 'this circuit here now', but is about how *a* current is produced by *a* voltage across *a* resistance. Teaching about gravity is about *a* force exerted on *a* mass; later on this is expanded to fields in general, to *a force* exerted by *a field* (gravitational, electric, magnetic) on *a test object* (mass, charge, current). An example of such very general schematic distinctions between kinds of explanations is the distinction between chemical and physical change. In what follows, the teacher (Leon) is seeing whether Year 9 students can identify this difference between prototypes of change.

Sally: Well we put a little bit of copper sulphate in both of them and then in one of them we put iron filings – and a thermometer in it as well – and in the other one we put magnesium powder and also put a thermometer in it.

Leon: Can I just say something, Sally, before you carry on? What was the reason for putting the thermometer in at all? What were you sort of suspecting?

Sally: The heat – um – made the red stuff in the thermometer to rise.

Leon: So you thought the temperature might go up?

Sally: Yes, that's it.

Leon: Because, what were you expecting to happen between the copper sulphate and the iron, and the magnesium and the copper sulphate – what did you think might happen between them? [*no answer*] What sort of reaction, what sort of change, gives out, often gives out a lot of energy?

Sally: Chemical.

Leon: Chemical. And you had some reason to think there might be, that there was a possibility of, a chemical reaction was going to happen here?

Sally: Yes.

Leon: So that's why you put the thermometer there?

Sally: Yes.

Leon: Good, now off you go.

Sally: And um – the heat did go up and [ ] at the start, the thermometer read 20 and then it went up to 30, and then er [ ] when we'd finished that one, it was clear in the middle so there was iron filings right at the bottom – and then clear – and then a few other iron filings at the top. Er [ ] and we also noticed a colour change in the iron filings – they were grey to start with and then they went a sort of reddish colour. And then the magnesium powder um [ ] also started at 20 and went up to 60, then went back down to 33. And as it was going up and down, it was bubbling and it was quite hot and had steam coming out, then it went green – and that's it.

Leon: OK. Do you conclude that it was a chemical or a physical change?

Sally: Er – yes.

Leon: Which one?

Sally: Er – chemical.

Leon: What was your evidence for the chemical change?

Sally: Er – steam coming out and it being hot and bubbly.

Leon: Anything else?
Sally: Colour.

We at once notice the distance between the worlds invoked here. Sally talks mainly in the here and now ('hot and bubbly', 'went up to 60') and of what she *saw*. Leon is talking much more generally about types of change. The bridge between them is the attention, evidently expected and clearly given, to a temperature change and to a colour change – both symptomatic of but not defining of a chemical change. Sally moves between this somewhat general level and the particular ('a colour change in the iron filings – they were grey to start with and then they went a sort of reddish colour'); this being a change she sees as one 'in the iron filings' which Leon would see as a chemical change – reddish copper coming out of the compound copper sulphate. Sally noticed that the blue solution went clear but did not associate that with the removal of copper.

Here we have the beginning along a long road towards understanding different forms of explanation. The immediate props for understanding are simplified (transformed) versions of the chemist's distinction – temperature and colour change. The gap is at its most evident when Leon asks, 'what did you think might happen between them?', but isn't answered. His repair job to the question provides a heavier clue, to which Sally can respond. What we think we see here is practice in thinking in parallel in two ways, one particular and one prototypical. It is from the rough edges between them – the 'semiotic friction' we mentioned in Chapter 2 – that Sally and her listening classmates can learn.

To conclude, we return to the subject matter with which we began – digestion – to illustrate that general prototypical kinds of change need not just to be abstracted but also to be instanced. Here is the teacher, David, making sure that 'digestion' does not remain *only* a prototype; that what 'digestion' is in particular is also made vivid, immediate and concrete.

David: So right – here [*points at dissected rat*] here is the stomach – yeah?
– and the food, when it's liquid, gets squirted into the first little bit of the tube there, which is called the duodenum . . . the duodenum is where extra digestive enzymes get squirted onto the food to help – to make – digestion continue.

Chapter 4

REWORKING KNOWLEDGE

Transforming knowledge

In Chapters 2 and 3 we have tried to show the work which the science teacher has to do in building a shared arena, in which the work of explanation can happen. Now our focus changes somewhat; now we wish to show a number of ways in which knowledge is transformed. This may be 'common-sense' knowledge already held by students from the experiences of everyday life; it may be the kind of knowledge that has been gradually built in the science classroom; or it may be the knowledge which has been produced by the scientific community, which is now transformed into 'school knowledge' appropriate for the students in this class.

We argue that knowledge is always transformed in the telling. Starting from scientific knowledge in the scientific community, we show how that knowledge is transformed into school science. We then consider a special kind of reworking of knowledge, in the creation and passing on of encapsulated stories about scientific work, stories which carry particular messages about science and scientific knowledge. Finally, we discuss the role of analogy and metaphor in scientific explanation and in explanations produced for, and by, students. In our telling of this story in this chapter, talk and knowledge, language and science, are often indistinguishable because we see them as deeply interdependent: talking as remaking knowledge, science as reshaping language.

Change and constancy

A central fact about languages is that, despite their appearance of stability and constancy, they are constantly changing. The source of change is clear: every act of communicating, every production of a meaningful sign, every understanding reached, is newly made. Every new-made meaning differs, however slightly, from the old one. Languages both change and stay the same because communicating necessarily implies both newness and sameness. Signs get meaning from their contrasts with others, yet make those contrasts anew each time. The source of constancy is thus also clear: new meanings are only possible by contrast with old ones.

Scientific knowledge is also continuously changing. The 'amount' of scientific knowledge has been estimated to double every fifteen years. But it is also the case that at a given moment, scientific knowledge appears to be very stable, providing a settled framework for understanding the world. And this framework is what schools see themselves as teaching. The dynamics of constancy and change in knowledge are rather like those of language. Constancy there has to be because every piece of knowledge depends on other knowledge. Change there inevitably is, because of the drive to new understandings.

A language community has to have ways of keeping its language both fixed and fluid. Similarly, a scientific community has to have ways of keeping its knowledge stable and constant, not to freeze it forever but – almost paradoxically – so that change is inevitable. One of the mechanisms of stability is schooling. It is no accident that in schooling knowledge is heavily policed; that 'right' and 'wrong' ways of thinking are sharply demarcated and differently rewarded. But this is not the whole story. Every telling, and every hearing, makes a little difference. Learning is an active construction; just because the knowledge of one person can appear in another does not mean that it was piped across – with the implication that it travels unchanged. *To teach is to act on other minds, which themselves act in response.*

Knowledge in the teaching thus differs from knowledge in the making. Scientific knowledge, as stabilized in the scientific community, has to be radically transformed before its form is fitted to a given act of teaching. And in the learning it is transformed again, as students make their own sense of it. All these transformations happen not by chance, but through work. Thus an account of knowledge transformation is best thought of as an account of the reworking of knowledge.

Knowledge made and transformed

There is a long path from the production of knowledge in the scientific community to its eventual appearance in the classroom (or in the Sunday newspapers). The history goes something like this. Fragments of possible 'knowledge in the making' are produced in original papers in the primary journals. Meetings at conferences expose new ideas and look for any emerging consensus on which results look right and which wrong. After some time, articles in review journals attempt to integrate results, to show how they relate, and to sift the reliable from the unreliable. Later still, monographs appear, often written by leaders in the field, which construct as complete a framework as possible, with the double purpose of archiving what is known, and of presenting it for the first time in a form designed to be learnable – mainly for the benefit of postgraduate students and of others wishing to enter the field. In due course, the material may be deemed suitable for undergraduate courses, at which point textbooks begin to appear, replete with problems and examples for the student. The first texts to appear have to rework the subject matter, ordering and framing it for the new audience. Later texts generally follow the formats thus established. Finally, the material is deemed fit for the school curriculum, and school textbooks incorporate it, often by drawing on previous university textbooks. Other textbooks copy the first ones (often including their errors together with some new ones). Just sometimes, ultimately, the material might become such a matter of common knowledge that it is not thought worth teaching at all since everybody knows it.

The whole process takes a very variable amount of time. The germ theory of disease more or less penetrated to everyday common sense within a century; the nature of inheritance through DNA reached the secondary school curriculum in one generation; the theory of electromagnetic radiation has still not yet got below the level of university courses despite being well over a century old. In the late nineteenth century Maxwell wrote letters complaining of the difficulty of teaching Newtonian mechanics to undergraduates; teachers now write letters to journals bemoaning the same difficulties in teaching the same thing to 14 year-olds.

There is a second, very different, path by which knowledge enters society. Technologies develop and people interact with their products. Some technologies use and depend upon existing theories – for example, radio transmission. But some technical practices (for example, smelting and metalworking) become fully established long (perhaps centuries) before they are understood – and some are, of course, still not understood. All technologies also contribute their own special kind of knowledge (a recent example is computer science).

Often technologies diffuse socially much more rapidly than does the knowledge behind them. Examples include radio and television, the widespread availability of electrical power, and the spread of computing. As a result, people generally have some first-hand acquaintance with a wide range of artefacts, without 'understanding' them. They may know more about an area through technological interaction than through knowledge of principles or mechanisms: an obvious example is preventing the decay of food by refrigeration or canning. These technical resources become available for teaching the knowledge behind them, and make evident by their existence the need for that knowledge.

The social consequences of this flow generate new needs in the educational system. Technological change alters the economy, and with that the skill and knowledge demands made by jobs, so that the educational system is expected to prepare people for coping with such jobs. Technological change thus helps to determine priorities for and the speed of transformation of knowledge.

Didactic transposition

The transforming of knowledge from forms which are appropriate to a given scientific community to forms adapted to teaching at a given level has – in the Anglo-Saxon educational tradition – no accepted name. Being unbaptized, it seems not to exist. In other European educational cultures, it has acquired the name 'didactic transposition'.

> The use of the term 'didactic' may need a gloss for the English reader, to whom it is likely to suggest 'unduly authoritarian teaching'. In a wide range of other European languages, 'didactics' refers to the careful analysis of subject matter for teaching purposes. What in England and the USA would be called 'science education' would there be called 'didactics of science'. To claim the title 'didactician' is a proud boast, not in the least an apology.

Let us take a very simple example of this reworking of knowledge for teachers and learners. It is the notion, widely used in primary science, of a 'fair test'. Faced with trying to communicate something of 'scientific method' at the primary level, primary teachers and their advisers hit on this expression of part of what is involved, and it proved so apt both for teachers and pupils that it caught on like wildfire. The idea transforms an aspect of what is done in doing science in such a way as to be memorable, intelligible and able to be put to use in the primary school.

What is explained in a science lesson is a carefully versioned form of knowledge, specially adapted to be appropriate for learners in a particular context. This versioning is the product of work, often over many years, by teachers and textbook writers. The process is in many ways akin to what the popularizer of science has to do to reach a mass audience, though the social constraints differ importantly – readers of popular science do not have to sit examinations!

One obvious product of didactic transposition is the circuit board now widely used in schools to teach about simple electric circuits. Another is the use of universal indicator to teach the idea of the pH (acidity or alkalinity) of a solution, just by associating colours of the indicator with the pH of the solution. A more complex example is the development of periodic table displays showing graphically such properties as ionic radii and ionization energies, so that various kinds of periodicity could be appreciated and compared visually.

In what follows we will examine another case in detail, showing some of the transformations that have been made and how they set the frame for the act of explaining in the classroom.

Seeing sound: a didactic transposition

In a lesson discussed in greater detail in Chapter 7, the teacher – Alan – is showing Year 8 students the patterns of sounds made into a microphone when they are displayed on a cathode-ray oscilloscope. He stresses *visualization*, a transposition from one medium, sound, to another, light. He is concerned about the relation between what is represented on the screen and the sound itself:

Alan: The sound waves we see on the screen – are they anything like the real sound waves that travel through the air? Can it display them as they really are?
Student: No.

The image is a bright line on a screen, and sound is not a bright line on a screen. So the representation is a long way from the represented. But in fact the answer 'Yes' would have been a good one too, since we can see more of the sound 'as it really is', than we can get from hearing it – for example the pattern of its variation in time. Alan continues his concern with the gap between representation and represented:

Alan: The cathode-ray oscilloscope can't display them like that, so how does it try to display the different types of sound?
Student: . . . by making different lines and different shapes.
Alan: OK, different lines – different shapes. You should see – if we get a nice pure note – you should see a nice smooth wave like that going across the screen.

By 'a nice smooth wave' Alan no doubt means a sinusoidal variation, which will be as dominant in the further discussion as it is rare in real life.

A variation in *time* has been transformed into a static visual display. And what is being looked at has a new name, a *wave*. But the students are not looking at a wave; they are looking at an oscillation graphed on the screen. Alan has substituted one picture for another which can be made, can be talked into seeming, the same. He now starts to put a lot of effort into the reciprocal relationships between wavelength and frequency. He capitalizes on the fact that they *saw* an effect on the appearance of the image, to avoid dealing with frequency and wavelength as variables having a reciprocal relation. That relation appears as 'higher means more squashed together' and the converse. Perhaps he thinks this is a big enough advantage to justify blurring what the image actually represents.

It is striking how physical and visual the language used is (see Chapter 7). A mere pattern of light on a screen has become objectified: 'they're all getting close together'. What Alan seems to be trying to do is to make as concrete as possible, 'present to us here and now', the protagonists of a new story about sounds. And that new story seems to have little to do with sounds as they appear to us in everyday life. It is all about vibrations, frequencies and wavelengths, and about patterns to be seen in wavy lines.

How does sound present itself in everyday experience? For the most part, sounds are just present to us, on a par with tastes and smells. We have little sense that they involve *vibration* (though we do sense vibrations for loud low-pitched sounds, and we do associate some sounds with vibration as in the rumble of traffic). We have little sense that sounds *travel* (even an echo or a delayed thunderclap appears to be 'a sound happening a little bit late'). For most purposes, a sound seems to be heard at the instant that it is made. The region round a source of sound appears to us to be filled with its sound. We often hear round corners. But it does seem that sounds can be blocked, since we hardly hear sounds from inside closed spaces. And the region filled with sound is rather local, since we do not often hear sounds from far off.

Living with technological artefacts teaches us that sounds can be recorded and played back, and that they can be sent by other means (telephone, television and radio). Experience does not tell us whether the air, which is always there, is an essential or accidental accompaniment to the possibility of making and hearing sounds. And since we have rare experience of deafness, and then mostly at second hand, being able to hear seems natural and normal, not in need of being made accountable.

What, by contrast, does the scientific story look like? Sounds are made by making vibrations. But for most sounds the vibrations are too rapid to feel as vibrations (typically from hundreds to thousands of vibrations per second). Sounds are heard by producing vibrations in bones in the ear, which set neurones firing and sending information about the vibrations to the brain. That information is subtly coded, so that we hear the presence of differently pitched sounds simultaneously (technically, the ear–brain system does Fourier analysis, unlike the eye–brain system with which we do not 'see' the different colours in the light from a source).

Sounds belong to a wide class of phenomena named 'waves', which share a similar underlying theoretical analysis – the equations describing them have similar forms, and the mechanisms are analogous. Because of this, there are a common set of terms to describe any wave:

- frequency (rapidity of vibration)
- wavelength (distance apart in space of correspondingly excited places)
- amplitude (magnitude of the maximum excitation at a point)
- velocity (speed at which the excitation propagates)

These and other terms are taught because wavemotion and vibration of many kinds have turned out to be important in many parts of science and engineering. The description of sound waves contributes to a much larger agenda than it seems. But while they are generalized terms of description, however, these terms also have explanatory force. The pitch of a sound 'is nothing other than' its frequency of vibration. The loudness of a sound 'is nothing other than' its amplitude of vibration.

A wave is a travelling disturbance. It is motion in motion (or more generally change in motion). There is *nothing* static about it. It changes simultaneously in time and space. To visualize waves, their motion has to be frozen so that what is unchanging can be contemplated. This is done in

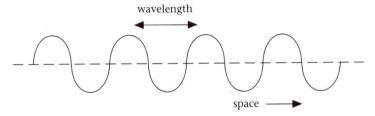

Figure 4.1 A wave frozen at a moment of time

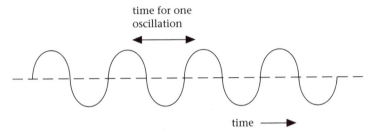

Figure 4.2 Oscillation in a wave at a point in space

two main ways: by freezing time as in a photograph to see the spatial pattern, or by giving time a spatial representation.

If space or time are represented spatially across the page, a way to represent the changes in pressure in the wave is to use the vertical spatial direction. This gives two now purely spatial and wholly static representations of something entirely dynamic. Figures 4.1 and 4.2 illustrate the two representations: one a wave frozen in time and the other oscillations at a single point in space. Note that (labelling apart) the diagrams look exactly the same. *The appearance is the same, but the meaning is quite different.* It is Figure 4.2 which Alan's students were seeing, with a microphone connected to an oscilloscope. What is on the screen is *not* a wave. It is a representation of an *oscillation*. The representation spatializes both time and intensity. It transforms a pattern of change in time into a static pattern in space. Because a representation of a sound wave in space, frozen at an instant, can look exactly the same, it is natural to speak of it as wave, however. But if we like, since the travelling of the wave itself correlates times and places, we could choose to 'read' the image as one showing how the wave *would* look if spread out in space.

The point of this rather lengthy analysis is to stress the amount of work and the complex detail involved in, the work of transforming knowledge which is needed even for what seems the simple matter of teaching about sound. Explaining sound requires explaining several kinds of representation, their relationships, and their relation to what is going on in the material process of making a sound. What can be written down as one or two equations is reworked into a variety of activities, visual experiences, and ways of talking.

In Chapter 5, on demonstrations, we discuss how material things become semiotic objects – signs as well as substance. The oscilloscope here is a clear example. Its very function is to make meaningful displays out of material things (sounds, electrical impulses) fed to it.

Explanatory icebergs: filling up atoms with electrons

Didactic transformations hide knowledge at least as much as they expose it. Explanations are like the tips of icebergs, with a large amount of supporting knowledge lurking below the surface.

We give an example taken from a series of lessons on the chemical periodic table, discussed later from a different point of view in Chapter 6. In this sequence, as in many textbooks, atoms are described as having layers ('shells') which may be successively 'filled up' with electrons. (Later in this chapter we will also consider 'filling up' as an example of metaphor.) The first shell can take two electrons, the second can take eight, the third either eight or eighteen and so on. Real differences between real substances such as sodium and sulphur, to everyday reason 'just how things are', are determined by these number patterns. Sodium is 'sodium' and sulphur is 'sulphur' because of the number and arrangement of electrons they possess.

The reader may well have the feeling that this talk of numbers – of the magic sequence 2–8–8 or 18, is far from being a full explanation. And this feeling is entirely correct. Plainly such numbers themselves call for explanation. It may be useful to sketch what this explanation is so that one can see the hidden part of the explanatory iceberg which underlies the above very common didactic form of explanation.

The only sensible or satisfying number of electrons which could 'fill' something is, plainly, simply *one*. And indeed at bottom this is the simple rule underlying this whole complicated scheme. It is that only one electron can be in a given state in the same atom. All the magic numbers are combinations of the number 1. The more complex number patterns arise because the 'state' of an electron depends on the shape of its distribution in space. Further, two electrons can occupy the same spatial distribution as long as they differ in the direction of their 'spin', up or down. This lets *two* electrons occupy each spatial distribution. The electrons fill up the spatial distributions in order of their energy, lowest first. The first two (giving the initial 2 in the magic sequence) occupy a spherically symmetric pattern close to the nucleus of the atom. The next set of possible spatial distributions is a bit more complicated. It has one spherically symmetrical pattern, but space being three-dimensional, there are a further three asymmetrical lobed patterns oriented in three directions at right angles. Thus this set of states can be occupied by two plus three times two electrons – eight in all. The later larger numbers (18, 32) arise from yet more complex spatial patternings of states. But in the end, all these numbers follow from three simple numbers: *one* for the number of electrons able to occupy one state; *two* for the number of spin directions; and *three* for the number of dimensions of space.

The didactic transposition from the quantum theory account above to one of 'filling' of 'shells' replaces its simplicity by magic and unexplained numbers. But it does retain something of the deep idea of the original, in the seemingly common-sense notion of 'filling'. In the quantum theory, the everyday notion of 'solid object' in which two such things cannot be in the same place at once is transmuted into the type of particle called 'fermions', no two of which can be in the same state at once. Deeply, the concept of the fermion explains the solidity of matter. It is rather typical of transposed notions that they retain such deep structure without this being easily able to be made explicit.

Stories, parables and narratives

The reworking of knowledge discussed above is of a conceptual kind. It is a reworking of the 'internal' organization of knowledge. Another kind of reworking is of the form in which we meet it, or in which it is represented to us. An example is embedding knowledge in stories, tales and narratives. Here is an instance:

> *Leon*: Who's going to watch that programme about that Russian – was she really a Russian? – who's going to watch that? – 'Anastasia' – Are you going to watch that? It's – er – they're doing – you should watch it, it looks quite fascinating [ ] You know they said they killed all the Tsar family in 1917 – right? – there's this woman in America – I think it was – since she says, 'No I wasn't killed' for some reason – obviously she was alive so she wasn't – but they didn't kill her right? – and it was a debate went on for years and years and years as to whether or not she really really was the Tsar's daughter. So what they've actually done is – now that she's dead – they've taken a bit of a bone – yes? – and looked at the DNA – you know now the DNA – and on the programme this week they're going to reveal on *Equinox* [a television programme] whether she really is – they can now – do you understand they can now? – go to the bones of the people who were killed and see if – because if she's their daughter it's going to be exactly – it's going to match. So it's going to be a fascinating programme I think.

At one level Leon is seeking to enliven things for his Year 10 class through a story. Stories are easy to remember because one part readily evokes the next, and the need for resolution which the narrative structure sets up, involves us as hearers and readers, willy-nilly. But at a deeper level we can think of the story as a 'knowledge carrier'. Some essential facts about DNA, that it is present in all cells, and that it is the material of heredity, are built into the structure of the story, together with other knowledge (e.g. DNA survives in dead bodies). Conceptual connections are carried by narrative links. Not all such stories used in explanations are so dramatic – here is a much more mundane example from a Year 8 lesson about sound:

Alan: Now then I used to have terrible problems using a phone box because I worked up in Scotland in a little village . . . where the Glenfiddich whisky comes from – so it was a bit nice. And when I used to phone home there used to be a great big clock tower in the middle of the village and throughout the summer they would have a piper standing next to the telephone boxes playing the bagpipes so you can imagine what that was like when you were trying to phone home.

The fact about sound, that it can travel through solid materials, is neatly carried by the story. Telephone boxes are of their nature enclosed, and one telephones from inside, so the very structure of the story, simple as it is, embodies the idea. The telephone box should have shut out the sound but it didn't.

In the next example, Leon (in a lesson about microbes) gets the Year 7 class to help create a small scenario to encapsulate some basic facts about microbes:

Leon: Picture this then – because this has happened to me – might have happened to you – this is a confession for my part. If you get some sliced bread, yeah? [ ] It's OK if you live in a big family, because you're eating it all the time right? – yeah – but I don't live in a big family, right, so I get – I get some sliced bread right? And it lasts quite a long time but usually I don't actually get to eat the last few slices – and you've got to tell me why I don't normally eat the last few slices of my – of a sliced loaf in my house. Can you tell me why?

Leon gets the answer he wants, that the bread goes mouldy, and this little episode now helps to carry the idea that unseen microbes are everywhere and in time will grow on anything which nourishes them. His students get the point. Two of them immediately recall parallel events:

Student: My uncle – ages ago – he left his packed lunch box and he went on holiday and he left it in his packed lunch box and when it was time to go all the . . .

Leon: You lift your lid off the Tupperware and you sort of go 'ugh'

Student: At our primary school you used to have these cupboards and you used to put our lunch boxes and then people used to leave it over night and all the damp . . .

In the next chapter, on demonstrations, we claim that stories like these have some of the character of demonstrations. We see that knowledge can be reworked into story-like forms, not merely to add to its 'liveliness' or 'interest', and not merely to show it 'applied' to some real context, but more fundamentally to act as an involving, a memorable and efficient knowledge carrier. The story *is* the knowledge, in a reworked form.

Moral tales or parables

Quite commonly, ideas about the nature of science are carried in moral tales or parables. Parables carry an idea about how things are or should be. Scientific parables carry ideas about how science is or ought to be. Archimedes leaping from his overflowing bath with a cry of 'Eureka', or Newton noticing the fall of an apple are part of the folklore of science. Unlike many other such tales, these two are unusually puzzling. The *moral* to be drawn does not seem obvious. Surely Archimedes knew that baths overflow; even more surely must Newton have known that apples fall from trees. Curiously, both serve the same ideological interest, but one which is often missed in the telling, perhaps because it is too uncongenial. *It is that one may make discoveries by taking pure thought.* In the case of Archimedes, it is that the volume of any object, however complex in shape, can be easily calculated by noting the rise in level of water in a container when the object is immersed in it. In the case of Newton, the theoretical insight is yet more startling. It is that the fall of an apple is just the same phenomenon as the 'fall' of the Moon towards the Earth as it circles the Earth; that one scheme is enough to embrace the motion of both heavenly and mundane objects. That idea changed Western culture for ever.

Science teachers, and science texts, regularly repeat such tales, often with their ideological point driving and shaping the telling: Fleming's discovery of penicillin; Kekulé's idea about the structure of benzene; Rumford boiling water by boring cannon endlessly; Einstein impressed by the Michelson–Morley experiment (of which in fact he had not heard). Again and again, serious historical investigation of these 'well-known' episodes shows that the parables are carefully shaped pieces of ideology, bending the facts in the service of a particular moral. As they are told, their tone is often unproblematic and confident, with little of the subtle qualification and contestation to be found in the writing of historians.

Let there be, however, no misunderstanding. A notion of how things ought to be cannot avoid ideology. It *is* ideology. Such parables capture broad world views, and broad world views are both important and necessary. We are *not* using the term 'ideology' in a derogatory sense.

The destruction of Vital Force: a parable in the classroom

A Year 11 class is beginning the study of organic chemistry. We discussed an earlier part of this lesson in Chapter 2. The teacher, Elaine, tells the well-known parable of the start of organic chemistry in its modern form, as the chemistry not of life but of carbon. Elaine had previously asked them what the word 'organic' meant to them, getting answers mainly to do with 'life'.

Elaine: Now originally, before about 1825 which probably seems like the beginning of the world to you, 1825, it's not even two hundred years ago, people like you did just now thought that there was a whole class of chemical substances that were special in some way because they were concerned with living things. In fact, they thought that these chemicals couldn't be made in a laboratory – they couldn't be made in test tubes and beakers and so forth – or in factories, although the industry wasn't organized in factories and we didn't have firms like –um– Glaxo and so on and ICI – they thought that these special chemicals could only be made inside living things or they were the waste products of living things or the decayed products of living things. In fact, they had a theory called the Vital Force Theory. Anybody know what 'vital' really means?

Student: 'Important'.

Elaine: How important?

Student: Major.

Elaine: How major?

Student: Extremely important.

Elaine: Extremely, so important that in fact

Student: It's life or death.

Elaine: life or death.

. . .

Elaine: 'Vital' is really concerned with something living – OK – so the Vital Force Theory says that to put these chemicals together, you needed this mysterious Life Force. It could only be done inside living things because you needed this mysterious Life Force. It's no good mixing things in beakers or test tubes, wouldn't work. Then along came a guy called Wöhler [ ] who I guess was German, maybe Austrian, I guess he was German – and he quite accidentally made a chemical substance in the laboratory and that chemical substance was called urea. Now you must have come across that before. What's urea?

Student: [*Inaudible*]

Elaine: It's a substance that dissolves in water that we call urine, and it's most definitely organic in the old sense. Because it's a waste product of living things, it's the way we get rid of our waste nitrogen compounds. So, he made urea, he wasn't trying to make this, he was trying to make something else and during the process he was heating it and it rearranged itself and it came out as urea. Well that upset the apple-cart a little bit didn't it? And lots of people didn't believe that he'd really made it and there was a lot of discussion but other people did think, 'Maybe there's something in this,' and after a little while, several of these organic compounds were made in laboratories. So we had to rethink – I say 'We' – I wasn't really alive in 1825, I wasn't really part of it. We had to rethink the theory. What we know

now, is that although many of these things are concerned in some way or another with living things, with animals and plants, and their waste products and their decayed products, and we include things like protein and carbohydrate, cellulose which makes the cell walls of plants – what they all have in common is they are carbon compounds. [ ] So can you write that in your books please. 'Carbon compounds.'

The ideological moral here is twofold. The first is the power of a single crucial event to overturn a whole theoretical world view. The second – a more difficult and reductionist moral – is that the chemistry of living things is nothing but the chemistry of carbon compounds. And that this is 'what we know now'. *This* is what you 'write in your books please'. The old view was *wrong* and we are *right*. The parable is forceful and heroic – 'massive misapprehension overthrown by seized-upon chance'. The parable also has messages about science as a human product, and the need for communal consensus. It is presented almost as a contemporary tale, using 'we' not 'they'. However, the key element which no teacher would leave out is that Wöhler made by accident a substance it was thought impossible to make. The focus on a person (as also in the thumbnail portraits of 'scientists' common in textbooks), serves to authorize the explanation, through attaching it to an authority.

We may also usefully refer here to a point put briefly in Chapter 1 and elaborated in Chapter 6, that explanations exist on many scales. Elaine's use of this parable gives a large-scale explanatory frame to all the explanations to come in lessons over several weeks – for some students over several years – about the chemistry of carbon. It explains why there is a subject of this kind to be learned, and why it is called 'organic chemistry'.

Analogy and metaphor

One obvious way of reworking knowledge is through analogy. Here is an example of a teacher using an analogy to make a subtle and crucial issue – electrons 'filling' shells in atoms – seem as simple and obvious as possible.

> *Ruth*: I try to imagine it like chairs really in an assembly hall. [ ] If you go into assembly the year leader she makes you go in row by row. When the first row is full you go into the next row. You don't tend to sit wherever you like.

We have already referred to this Year 10 lesson above, and it is discussed further in Chapter 6. The analogy is not about any one atom. It is about imagining making an atom by successively adding electrons, or, equivalently, about how to make 'correct' pictures of the arrangement of electrons in atoms. At all events, some strange knowledge is made familiar and 'easy' to grasp. Here the work of reworking knowledge is evident to all concerned. Nobody would suppose that electrons in atoms have the equivalent of a 'year leader' enforcing the rules of their construction. In fact, the equivalent of the 'year leader' in the analogy is the student – who makes the marks representing electrons in atoms go in their assigned places.

At an opposite extreme, analogy or metaphor may be so well hidden – so taken for granted – as not to seem to be analogy or metaphor at all. Clive Sutton in his book *Words, Science and Learning* provides a wealth of examples. One is that of 'cell' in biology, introduced by Robert Hooke when he looked at cork through the microscope and saw tiny structures arranged like the cells of a honeycomb. Another is 'molecule' meaning 'tiny lump'. The list is endless, and for a good reason. Making new knowledge can only be done by reworking old knowledge. With help from William Whewell – who himself coined the word 'scientist' – Faraday exploited Greek words to invent the terms 'ion' (traveller) and 'electrode' (path for electricity). And he did it not to have graceful expressions, but to *enforce a point of view*. Faraday wanted to build right into scientific language his notion that electrolysis was a matter of particles travelling in a solution carrying with them electricity which entered at one plate and left at another.

Science is not special in this respect. Everyday language is full of – some would say entirely composed of – metaphor, much of it hidden. The word 'language' itself – to do with tongues – is a case in point. So is 'metaphor' – a 'carrying across' of something, a metaphor used differently in the word 'transport'.

Our concept of didactic transposition invokes the very same process. The example of the multiple transpositions involved in the lesson on sound shows, on the one hand, the extent to which this has become 'entirely natural', and on the other the extent to which it is entirely essential.

Students thinking with analogy and metaphor

In Chapter 2 we gave the example of a teacher finding and bringing to attention a possible 'misconception', that melted wax is water. And in Chapter 3 we considered the same issue from the point of view of constructing the entity 'liquid'. Here we use the same discussion to show that part of what is at issue is analogy and metaphor. The teacher is Steve; the class is from Year 7.

Steve: It's liquid?
Pretesh: Yes.
Steve: Is that a different word for water?
Pretesh: Yeah.
Steve: Yeah. It's like water in some ways isn't it. What about it is like water? [*The teacher is swirling the liquid wax in a test-tube*]
Pretesh: It can, it, it, it can
Student: Sir, sir, sir.
Pretesh: it can move. It's runny.
Steve: It's runny, yeah, it's runny like water. What else is like water? In what ways is it like water?

Student: It's like thick water.

. . .

Steve: Shamar?

Shamar: It's liquid.

Steve: Right. Okay, it's a liquid, like water, it's a liquid like water. Can you just explain what you mean by that.

Shamar: It's like, um, it's runny.

Steve: It's runny. You can pour it [*teacher picks up test-tube*] you could pour it out of the tube. It's a liquid.

What is the issue here? Do the students think melted wax is 'really' water? When Steve asks later if they can drink it, they are clear that this would be unwise. But it *is* very much like water, both clear and runny. And 'watery' is a very common everyday way of saying 'liquid'. Steve capitalizes on that to compare melted wax and water, and so to provide a motive for the term 'liquid' which catches what they have in common. Without 'liquid' the word 'water' has to do service both for the drinkable stuff made of hydrogen and oxygen, and for watery substances.

Notice that here it is the students, not the teacher, who are the source of the analogy between melted wax and water. And we know that this kind of thing is going on all the time, underlying many of what are called 'alternative conceptions'. Our focus in this book is usually on 'teaching', because it is the teacher who provides the publicly available 'explanations'. But the same processes inform learning, even though they usually remain less visible and less audible.

Constructing new meanings

We mentioned above the important role played by analogy and metaphor in constructing new meanings within scientific work itself. A famous example is the way Darwin found his way to the theory of evolution by an analogy with domestic breeding of animals. The example is not an exception; analogy and metaphor are always crucial in the thinking of new thoughts and the having of new ideas. When they are new, as for instance in current thinking of the brain as like a computer, the existence of the analogical basis is clear. But when grown older and more familiar, as in thinking of influences spread through empty space as 'fields', the source metaphor is less immediately clear. Similarly, to think of both light and sound as 'waves' is to invoke an almost taken-for-granted analogy with what can be seen from the beach or felt in a boat.

It is tempting to suppose that the value of analogy and metaphor in learning science is somewhat superficial – to make ideas more palatable, more vivid, more accessible. Just as analogy and metaphor are commonly but wrongly thought of as 'grace-notes' of language, with a mainly decorative function, the 'real work' being done by plain literal expression, so it is all too easy to think of them as elegant or pleasing but inessential aspects of explaining scientific ideas. A view strongly present in Clive Sutton's book (see p. 71) is that attention to metaphor and analogy can enliven and humanize scientific thinking for students. No doubt all these effects are present, but we believe that the importance of analogy and metaphor in learning science is much more fundamental than this, and is similar in kind to their fundamental importance in doing science.

To conclude this chapter, we will give a few further broadly sketched examples of analogies and metaphors at work. First we will discuss those which are relatively visible – overt metaphors – and then those which are better hidden – covert metaphors.

Overt metaphors

An example of overt metaphor from the classroom (in Year 9) concerns the control of the hormone system, explained by the teacher using the metaphor of orchestration:

Leon: Does anyone here play a musical instrument?
Student: Yes.
Leon: Where did you play, at school or in a band?
Student: Orchestra.
Leon: Anyone else?
Student: Piano.
Student: I play the trombone.
Leon: What would happen if you'd all got together as a group of people and you could all play these instruments, and you just start to play?
Student: You get a racket.
Leon: There would be a racket. In order to control it and to make sure it all works and plays a tune, what do you need?
Student: A team.
Leon: To work as a team. You need a team. What does an orchestra usually have?
Student: A conductor.
Leon: A conductor and what does a conductor do?
Student: Controls the whole thing.
Leon: Yes, a conductor controls the whole thing. So, think about it. We've said ovaries, testes, adrenal glands, thyroids, Islets of Langerhans, if they were all doing their own thing, what would the body be like?
Student: A catastrophe.
Leon: It would be a bit of a mess. So, you can probably half guess that there is some sort of system controlling all the glands together. Some way of making sure that all switch on and switch off at the right time.

The analogy need not be at all complicated. In the next extract the teacher, Alan, organizes a whole Year 8 lesson around the eye thought of as a camera:

Alan: What I would like you to do please – if you look at the diagram of the eye you will see towards the front there something called a lens. Can you all find the lens on the diagram please, OK [ ] good. Now then I've got here a variety – a selection – of different types of lenses OK. They are obviously much larger than the lenses in your eyes but they work in exactly the same way. The lens in your eye is much cleverer if you like, because it actually changes thickness. It can become thicker and more powerful or it can become thinner like this one. So the lens in your eye is much cleverer but they basically perform the same sort of thing.

Here the eye is being reworked to be like a camera and a camera is being reworked to be like the eye. It is the tension between the two that has a chance to be productive. The experience of vision is one of 'simply seeing'. Nothing seems to come between looking and perceiving. The camera, by contrast, splits apart 'taking the picture' and 'looking at the image'. So the analogy can help in the difficult matter of thinking about vision from 'outside' the taken for granted experience of doing it.

In these examples, the analogy provides a framework within which productive questions can be asked and answers can be sought without needing to know everything. How do hormones control glands? What controls the controllers? And so on. The student can see better what may need to be thought about or understood. And the analogy may suggest a form of answer.

But this process, of seeing what more may need to be understood, is precisely the role of analogy and metaphor in scientific work itself. Darwin's analogy between evolution and domestic breeding immediately suggests the urgent question, 'What in evolution could act like the person selecting individuals from which to breed?' Thus Darwin was driven towards natural selection.

Analogy and metaphor work in this way by their suggestive and imaginative power. That power derives from their concreteness, which allows thought to get to work without yet knowing everything it needs to know. An analogy comes as a complete concrete package able to be envisaged as a whole. If DNA works like a zip fastener, what plays the role of the zip? If light is a wave, what corresponds to the water? If the brain is like a computer, where could its programmes come from? And so on.

Covert metaphor at work

Metaphor is often strongly but invisibly at work in scientific terminology and in scientific ways of talking and writing. Human reproduction provides a set of obvious examples: egg, ovaries, penis (Latin 'finger'), menstrual ('monthly'). Such terms are not at all arbitrary. Their invention is driven – motivated – by the specific interest of the maker of the metaphor, as we suggested in our example of Faraday's 'naming' of ions and electrodes. Metaphors are not neutral descriptions but strongly suggest images of 'how things are'. When

Hooke called the small parts of living material 'cells', the word at once suggests questions about what is inside, what their walls are made of, how stuff can get in or out, and so on. Here are some examples, taken from transcripts we have cited already, of words and of ways of talking doing such suggestive work.

The first two examples concern terms from the 'scientific way of talking' which use metaphor descriptively. In the first we should note that 'transparent' is *not* a 'better' word for 'see-through'; this is precisely what it means (Latin: *trans parare*, 'appear through'). In the second we need to recall that the term 'alkali' comes from Arabic science and refers to material obtained from potash – that is, the ashes of wood used to fire pots, which was used both as a fertilizer and with fats to make soap, the latter process making essential use of the property chemists call alkalinity.

> *Teacher*: ... this hot wax at the moment is like water because it's see-through. What is a better word for 'see-through'? A longer one.
> *Student*: Transparent.

> *Teacher*: Why do they call them alkali metals?
> *Student*: They make alkali.
> *Teacher*: Right. When it reacts with water it's producing some sort of solution that's alkaline.

The next example illustrates the rich associations a term – here 'organic' – can have, and the way metaphors evoke complexes of meaning. That complex is exactly what this teacher needs to get at in order to build some sympathy for a now-discredited theory – the Vital Force Theory – which she wants to use to introduce the subject of organic chemistry to a class (see pp. 68–70 for more of the context).

> *Teacher*: Any other ways you've met this word 'organic'?
> *Student*: Food.
> *Teacher*: Food. Right. [ ] Does it remind you of any other words you've come across in science?
> *Student*: Organism.
> *Teacher*: Organism. Alright. What is an organism?
> *Student*: A living thing.

So far we have concentrated on 'terms', on words. But there are metaphorical ways of talking as well, which shape ways of thinking. They also work in transforming knowledge. Consider the following:

> *Teacher*: It's got a coating like rust – it's oxidized, OK? It's got a coating on the surface where it's reacted with the air ... Look at that. There you can see a very very bright silver surface that is practically going grey. The air is reacting with it very fast indeed.
>
> *Student*: ... we put the egg on top and I think the pressure pulled it in.

> *Teacher*: Right. Yes. So we got a hard-boiled egg that we got into the bottle and we said that it had been pushed into the bottle by the air.

In the first, 'coating', 'rust', 'on the surface', 'reacting with the air' mutually reinforce one another (coatings are on surfaces, rust is a coating and is on surfaces, rust is the result of a reaction, the air reaches solids only at the surface) to build an image for the mind's eye. And it is an image from which the student can make immediate inferences: cover the surface to prevent the coating; scrape off the coating to get a reaction with air. In the second of this pair, there is a conflict of ways of talking and thinking. The sight of an egg drawn into a bottle as water vapour in the bottle cools and creates a partial vacuum is striking, and the natural way to see it is as the egg 'sucked' in, not 'pushed' in. So strong is this perception that the student says that the pressure 'pulled', even though pressures are things which press. The metaphorical force of the term 'pressure' is not enough to overcome the natural image of what is going on.

The next examples illustrate analogical ways of talking about things we cannot see directly, because they are too small or too big. The first is about lubrication in joints and the second is about the solar system:

> *Teacher*: . . . they're just rolling on these molecule-size ball bearings, yes? So do they get really hot and wear away? No, because I'm just rolling instead of scraping . . .

> *Teacher*: Why do the planets keep going round the Sun? Are they joined onto the Sun?
> *Student*: No.
> *Teacher*: Not in any way. So what actually keeps them going round? Why don't they just go off by themselves? Why do they stay in those nice little orbits?

In the first, the teacher transforms molecules into ball-bearings, to help imagine how oily substances do the job of lubrication. In the second, there is again a conflict. It is easy to imagine that planets 'follow' ('stay in') their predestined ('nice little') orbits as if the orbits were railway tracks. But there are no tracks, and nothing like a string joining planets to the Sun to serve as an alternative. Here the metaphorical level of thought is being undermined so as to make a need for another image.

The examples in this section make it plain that analogy and metaphor are not merely decorative or helpful, a kind of aid to thinking for those who find it difficult. They *are* thinking. And they *are* the making of meaning.

Chapter 5

DEMONSTRATION: PUTTING MEANING INTO MATTER

What *is* demonstration?

In this chapter we consider an aspect of explanation which is essential to science, namely demonstration. There is a long tradition of demonstration in science teaching – a tradition especially strong in Germany but important everywhere. Companies manufacture and market large amounts of equipment for demonstrating everything from magnetism to microwaves; from cell preparations to colloids. 'Great demonstrators' are remembered with affection and awe; they include several famous names from the history of science such as Faraday and Tyndall.

It seems obvious that demonstrations are simply a matter of 'showing nature as it is', as clearly and vividly as possible. We are going in this chapter to cast some doubt on this seemingly self-evident proposition. We will argue that the key aspect of demonstrating is to coerce material phenomena into being meaningful. What that statement might mean will gradually become clear.

We can gain an entry into the argument by reporting a demonstration done by a teacher (Leon) in the course of a Year 8 lesson about light. Leon needs to explain that in a 'transverse wave' the wave energy travels at right angles to the oscillatory motion of the wave. We ask the reader to try to imagine the events which are happening here.

Leon: Where did the energy go? [ ] Do it this way [*singles out a pupil and instructs her as follows*] Hold this heavy rope. Hold it – heavy rope. Ready? Hold it tight [ ] [*clenches his hand in front of him to*

> *hold the other end of a rope and pulls towards himself*] I'm going
> to do the movement this way [*moves his head up to indicate the
> direction*] Right, are you ready? [*moves his clenched hand sharply
> up and down*] What happened to you? I'll do it really hard [*makes
> the movement again, more strongly*] What happened to you? You
> never moved [*moves his hand as the student's hand would have
> moved*] I'm doing this really hard. I'll do it one more go [*repeats
> the up and down movement again*] So which way did I move?

Student: You went up again.

Leon: But where did the energy – where does the energy go? Which
         way did it go? I moved this way [*gestures up and down*] but the
         energy went [*gestures from himself to the student*] that way.

When two people hold a rope between them, a sideways shake at one end
travels along the rope as a wave pulse, and can be felt as a sideways tug at
the other end. Many readers will have been able to envisage such an event
happening in this small demonstration.

Such demonstrations are entirely usual. *What makes this one unusual is that
there was no rope!* Leon merely mimed handing the end of a heavy rope to
the student, but with a convincing play of finding it heavy. He and the pupil
'held' the ends of the imaginary rope with strongly clenched hands, and
Leon made real up-and-down motions of his hand, 'watching' the imaginary
rope attentively to 'see' what would happen, following the 'wave pulse' with
his eyes. A demonstration of a real wave pulse on a rope has been turned
into an imaginative exercise in envisaging what should happen. It was a
demonstration in thought not in fact, but one made vivid and concrete by
the convincing actions and gestures. The language is entirely of the actual
and present ('Hold this heavy rope', 'I'll do it really hard', 'What happened
to you?'). It is not at all hypothetical – Leon does not say, 'Imagine we have
a rope. What would happen if . . . ?'

We think this little episode opens up some important questions about
what demonstrations are, and the role they play in explanation. Notice some
crucial features of Leon's demonstration (and we will call it that, despite the
temptation to place the term in scare quotes):

- the demonstration cannot go wrong
- what was 'shown' was events in the service of a theoretical conception
- what was 'seen' was shorn of accidental irrelevancies
- the talk was of unobservables (energy) as well as of observables
- every effort was made to dramatize the event as 'happening in front of us
  here and now'
- the talk emphasized not so much 'seeing as' as 'being as' (not 'How must
  we think of the energy as travelling?' but 'Which way did it go?')
- its function was to enforce a vision of some entities, including unobservable
  ones, as real constituents of the world
- it had a strong and irreducible imaginative element

We believe that – with some few qualifications – these features are generally
characteristic of demonstrations. They concern the world and its workings,

as some scientific theory envisages them to be. And Leon's imaginary demonstration raises the question whether it was better for him to do it this way rather than for real. We think that in this case there are good arguments – to do with the necessary role of imagination – why it was better.

We conclude this introduction with an (imaginary but all too familiar) evocation of a well-known demonstration as it *not* meant to be experienced by students:

> The teacher put two wires into some water in a little bowl. Froth grew on the water, and she scooped up a bit of the froth and put a match to it. The froth went bang! right there in her hand. But she wasn't hurt at all. I don't know what it was supposed to show but she must be very brave to do it.

Many a student has gone away from a demonstration saying, 'I don't know what it was supposed to show, but . . .'. The event is there but it lacks meaning. The student remembers what could be *seen*, but lacks an idea of what the events *are supposed to mean*. The teacher wanted to show water being torn apart by an electric current into hydrogen and oxygen, which then exploded, combining back into water and releasing the energy which had been supplied in tearing them apart. The student saw wires, water, froth and a bang. The demonstration failed in its effect on many counts in the list of features above, not least the imaginative, even though it 'worked'.

Vexing nature by art

Francis Bacon, a contemporary of Galileo, and so writing at the time when what we now call science was being invented, gave the following advice to observers of nature:

> . . . the secrets of nature reveal themselves more readily under the vexations of art than when they go their own way.
> Francis Bacon, *The New Organon*, Book One, XCVIII

What he had in mind was that in the events of the natural world, the effects of various entities are entangled with one another, so that the effect of the entity one wants to understand may be interfered with by the effects of others.

A good example from the history of science is the discovery of electrons by J. J. Thomson. In the late nineteenth century 'cathode rays', produced when electricity was discharged in gases at low pressure, were well known but their nature was a puzzle. Some thought they were a kind of immaterial radiation; others thought they were beams of charged particles. One piece of evidence against them being beams of charged particles was that they were not deflected by an electric field – as they should be if they consist of moving charges. Thomson had the idea that the problem was that a cloud of charge from the ionised gas shielded the cathode rays from the electric field, neutralizing its effect. So he progressively reduced the gas pressure, to reduce this effect, and ultimately found that he could deflect the cathode rays. What had seemed to be contrary evidence now became the result of a side-effect.

Thomson had to vex nature by art – to artfully remove one effect so as to see another. The point, of course, is completely general. Any experiment must be a carefully controlled and constructed artifice, built to reveal what it is built to reveal. The same, *a fortiori*, is true of demonstrations, of course.

The suggestion of circularity is unsettling. If an experiment or demonstration 'shows' only what it is 'meant to show', is it getting anywhere? The answer, however, is 'yes' because nature is recalcitrant. Experiments are not *bound* to work. Our theoretical fancies may turn out to be exactly that: fancies whose consequences cannot be made to manifest themselves. But what this brief argument does show is that in doing and in teaching science, experiment and demonstration both involve a tension between the theoretical and the material. Both are of the essence artful, contrived, 'made'. Yet both can fail in actual performance.

We suggested above, however, that demonstrations cannot fail, and must now explain what we had in mind. In fact, of course, every science teacher doing a demonstration is nervous of it failing. What is it to fail? It is that the demonstration does not show what it was meant to show. The problem is a failure of *meaning*. Nature has not been vexed as intended.

Teachers are very clear about this. David, teaching in Year 10 about plate tectonics, with a demonstration of convection in a jelly-like substance ready to show, anticipated its failure with a typical blend of gloom and insouciance:

David: . . . with a bit of luck, I should show you an experiment – undoubtedly it won't work . . . so we'll – we'll pretend that we're doing an experiment that might work.

. . .

David: . . . what this is meant to be actually – er – it's meant to be custard, but unfortunately we didn't have any custard, so we're trying it with gelatine, just to see if we can get it to work. But let's just explain what's here. This is a thick jelly-like mixture, then, you can see how thick it is [*turns large beaker on its side, and there is no flow of the substance*] OK? At the bottom here there is [*circles with his finger at the base of the beaker*] um – a blue layer, with a white layer on top. Now I'm going to try to heat that gently [*adjusts bunsen burner*] because what I want to show you is something we've talked about several times already, which is convection [*places the beaker on the tripod*] . . . I've just got this feeling that that stuff is so solid that the whole thing is going to crack.

. . .

David: What you should get is a convection current. What you're more likely to get – as I said, I've done this before with custard but we haven't got any custard – what you're more likely to get is some kind of nuclear custard explosion, and the whole thing stuck to the ceiling. [*Students laugh*] But with a bit of luck – with a bit of luck – what we should start to see – what we should see is the blue layer at the bottom starting to circulate. We should get a convection current starting, as the blue starts to rise and goes to the surface.

In fact the beaker did crack and any movement of the blue layer was at best marginal. In that sense, the demonstration failed. But the class had seen, in the context of learning about the structure of the Earth, something more or less 'solid' heated and expected to move. The point of the demonstration was not to make gelatine convect, but to make a parallel between convection and processes inside the Earth. The *meaning* was still clear: continents move because they are carried on hot moving molten rock circulating inside the Earth, and the underlying process is one which is familiar in everyday life, not something exotic. The demonstration offered a model for thought, not a slice of life. Here is a further example of the transformation of knowledge through analogy, discussed earlier in Chapter 4.

A demonstration, then, is an event in which some aspect of the material world is to be made meaningful in a particular preordained way. And this is done usually through special *apparatus*, chosen and constructed so as to exhibit the meaning as forcefully, clearly and unambiguously as possible. The demonstration does not put what is to be demonstrated at risk. Yet, making something 'really happen' is, because of the feeling of risk, more forceful in its effect than just saying that it will happen.

Demonstration apparatus and demonstration itself, are material objects and events *composed into meaningful signs*. The sign says that a particular theory is in good working order; that a given natural material process is to be understood as entities going through their expected behaviour; that things *are* as we *say* they are. At first sight it is not obvious that brute events in the material world are the kind of thing that *could* be made into a sign. Surely signs are parts of messages, not things which 'just happen'? Consider an air track: a hollow beam on which gliders 'float' on a cushion of air with hardly any friction. Set moving, such a glider travels an astonishing distance up and down the track, barely slowing down. It 'demonstrates' that if there are no forces, motion continues 'for ever', flatly contradicting the everyday belief that all movement needs a cause. We choose the example because of the transparency of its artifice. The air track is clearly a heavily manufactured human artefact, not something 'natural'. Its sharp linearity is evident to the eye; the small holes are carefully contrived. And why on earth should a glider supported mysteriously on air blown through holes in a beam be taken as *the representative* of 'a moving thing', rather than a football or a car? The example shows rather more clearly than most how a demonstration must be understood as *matter put in service of theory*.

We may say that the students *see* demonstrations as events of a particular kind because of the work the teacher puts into preparing them to see the events in that way. When we look at the character of that work, it is in large part a presentation of some theory. The students' perception is a product of the theory presented prior to the demonstration. The theory transforms events from an experience of wires, froth and bangs, into something quite different.

Alkali metals: meaning-making with matter

We turn now to illustrate, through an extended account of one demonstration lesson in Year 10, how a teacher can carefully shape a blend of talk, action and phenomena into a set of meanings. The example is a demonstration of the properties of three so-called 'alkali metals' – lithium, sodium and potassium.

Seen one way, the demonstration involves placing a small quantity of one substance in water, seeing what happens; placing a small quantity of another substance in water and seeing what happens; and then doing the same with a third substance. Put thus, there is no meaning. All we can guess is that three substances are to be compared, because the same thing is done to each. But these are not just any old substances. They have been chosen and ordered by the teacher with reference to their place in the periodic table.

> *Tom*: Good. What we've done so far is to colour in areas of the periodic table . . . What I want to do today is to go on to start, looking at each of these groups in turn. Now the one we're going to look at today is [*picks up a book containing a copy of the periodic table, and displays it to the students*] that one [*points to a column of the periodic table*] the one called number one, the one with lithium, sodium, and potassium in it, okay. So we can start off, by, giving you the name of that group, this is the title for today's lesson [*writes 'Alkali Metals' on the whiteboard*] Okay, the title underlined please.

What would have been bits of greyish stuff put into water here becomes a group of three elements, with names, and a group name (alkali metals). They belong to a *table*, and have *order*. We shall see in fact that the whole demonstration is organized in a 'tabular' way, down to the details of the teacher's actions.

Tom asks the students to write down observations in each part of the demonstration in table form, so that later the students find themselves observing not phenomena themselves, but similarities and differences between phenomena.

Tom now goes through a sequence of actions, using lithium. He draws attention to the fact that the lithium is stored in oil. He cuts a small piece with a knife, showing that it is quite hard to do so. He displays the silvery surface, and draws attention to the way that, as they watch, it slowly tarnishes. Then he puts some indicator in water in a dish, and drops the lithium in. He draws attention to the reaction, shown by bubbles forming and by a change of the indicator near the lithium to a colour indicating an alkaline product. He sets the gas from the bubbles alight with a match, and notes that hydrogen burns in the way that this gas (whatever it is) burns.

Table 5.1 Comparison of alkali metals

Element	Atomic number	Hardness	Surface	Tarnishes	Reacts with water	Solution	Produces
Lithium	3	hard	bright	slowly	gently	alkaline	hydrogen
Sodium	11	soft	bright	quickly	strongly	alkaline	hydrogen
Potassium	19	very soft	bright	very quickly	violent	alkaline	hydrogen
. . .							
Francium	87	liquid			explodes	alkaline	hydrogen

What is important is that when he comes to sodium, he repeats the same actions, in the same way, even to the point of doing each in the same place on the bench as the previous one. Here is part of what was said as Tom went through the first part of this exercise, while repeating it with sodium.

Tom: Now we're going to see what happens when we cut it. [*Cuts the sodium*] Right, look at how soft that is. Okay, so its softer,

Student: I've got harder.

Tom: [*Holds small piece in front of the class, with tweezers*] and it's going, it's going white very very fast indeed, much quicker than before.

Student: Going what?

Tom: Going white, it's oxidizing, or tarnishing much faster than the last bit.

Student: Is it hard sir?

Tom: No, it's soft, it's, it's like, it's now like hard butter. If you're cutting it with knife it's about the same toughness as hard butter.

We can see the previous steps replicated. Also, we can notice the built-in comparison ('softer', 'faster', 'it's now like . . .'). It is helpful at this point to show the tabular structure which, when one has watched the whole demonstration, emerges as the pattern underlying everything the teacher does (Table 5.1). This is a table about two things: resemblance and progressive difference. Some terms are the same and others vary. But the variations are variations on the same themes: all are cuttable but some more easily than others; all react with air and with water but some do it more rapidly than others. And these progressions match the numerical progression of atomic number, which in the end turns out to be the deep underlying point. It is the theoretical patterns of the periodic table which order the teacher's actions – he shows the elements in strict sequence. And the tests are never related to the character of the substances involved, but are seen to be significant simply for their consistency with the pattern in question. There is a strong focus in all the talk and in the patterned action on similarity with difference. Indeed Tom reinforces early on the point that the substances in question are theoretical entities. He questions the class about what they know of the atomic number, and of the numbers of protons and neutrons in the nuclei, of these three elements. All this, of course, concerns unobservables. There is no question of looking at these properties. In the demonstration, however, Tom represents what is going on as 'looking and seeing'. But, as we see in the next extract, what is 'observed' goes well beyond what is seen.

Tom: Right now then, we want to know what the gas is [lights a match] Let's have a look [moves lighted match to the metal on the water]
Student 1: Flameable.
Student 2: Flammable.
Student 3: Hydrogen.
Student 4: Hydrogen.
Tom: Right how do you know it's hydrogen?
Students: It pops.
Tom: It's popping, it's a gas that catches fire...
Student: Like the big airship.
Tom: It's quite, it's quite a horrible smell actually.
Student: I can't smell it.
Tom: It's like, it's like a choking sensation.

The gas 'pops' and catches fire. So does hydrogen. It does not of course follow that the gas is hydrogen. The actual argument going on here is that theory leads us to expect hydrogen, so we check for one of the things hydrogen does. Nature has been given a chance to come up to scratch and has done so. We can be rather sure that if the gas had failed to catch fire, Tom would have said something like, 'Well it should have ...'. Nevertheless, it did, and the story that the reaction makes hydrogen is underscored. As we suggested previously, in a way the demonstration cannot go wrong. It does not discover facts; it means that theories are in good shape.

We can see even more clearly the mingling of 'what happens' with its interpretation and meaning in the next discussion, about the observable fact that the indicator solution went purple near the lithium.

Tom: Okay, so you can say, it's turned, it turns the indicator purple. [Students cough]
Tom: It will soon clear. It turns the indicator purple, when the metal is added to water [ ] so can anyone now give me, er, a reason why you think they'd use that name for the Group I metals? Why do they call them alkali metals?
...
Tom: Right, when it reacts with water it's producing some sort of solution that's alkaline. Now what was in there beforehand?
Student: Green indicator.
Tom: Yeah, green indicator in [?]
Students: Water.
Tom: Water, okay, it was in water. So whatever has happened in the water now, it's gone alkaline. Okay, what gas was given off?

Students: Hydrogen.
Tom: Right, what do you get if you take some hydrogen away from water? What's left?
Student: Oxygen.
Tom: Oxygen yeah. OK so you'd, erm, what you've actually got left is one H and an O. One, water is H_2O, isn't it?
Students: Yes.
Tom: And one of the Hs has been nicked, or stolen, by what?
Student: Burning.
Tom: By the sodium, by the, sorry, by the lithium. Okay, so the, the lithium has st– stolen one of the, erm, one part of it for itself, the OH, and it's thrown the bit that it doesn't want, the hydrogen, out, so it's come off, as a gas, and we're able to set fire to it, okay? Let's have a look at the next one.

The mixture of kinds of inference and interpretation here is complex and interesting. The inference to alkalinity from colour change is done by making the colour change *mean* alkalinity. The teacher is very clear that colour changes of the indicator have meanings (see the highlighted remark below).

Tom: You've seen this before, this is called universal indicator – basically it's vegetable juice. What colour, what colour is it?
Student: Green.
Students: Green.
Tom: Green, okay. Now I put some, in the water. [*Puts some universal indicator in the water with an eye-dropper*]
Student: Some?
Tom: Just so the, okay, the water's gone green, yes? Okay, so, **what that means** is that the water, is neutral. Now what number is neutral on the pH scale? Can anyone remember?
Student: Seven.
Tom: Seven, good, right. Seven is neutral. If it went an acid what colour would the water go?
Student: Green.
Tom: Red. Suppose it went alkaline?
Student: Blue.
Tom: Blue. Okay, so we've got red at the acid end, blue, blue or purple at the alkali end, green in the middle. So whatever I put in there, if it changes the colour we'll be able to tell whether it's going acid or alkali, won't we?

Further support is sought, not from experiment, but from a theoretical interpretation which would make sense of the production of alkali. Here it is the argument that the pair OH – the signature of alkalis – is 'stolen' from water (HOH), leaving hydrogen to be evolved. And this interpretation is further buttressed by the way it requires the giving off of hydrogen, to occur – as has just been 'shown to be the case'. Theory expects; demonstration (hopefully) delivers.

We can here see rather clearly how an explanation is built like a story, with participants in the story each doing their predetermined thing. The demonstration starts from this story and tries to exhibit its events as actually occurring in front of us.

Earlier in this chapter we discussed demonstrations and demonstration apparatus as artifice, as 'designed to show'. But we also stressed the role of real events they produce, which – as students know very well – do not *have* to happen just because we say they will. Where, then, in this example of the properties of alkali metals, is the artifice? There is no elaborate equipment; just pellets of metal, a knife, matches, water and indicator.

The artifice, we argue, is in the deliberate patterning of behaviour. For each substance in turn, the teacher cuts it, inspects it for shine and tarnish, puts it in water, ignites the gas, and notes the indicator colour change. Just as physical apparatus embodies the theory it is made to 'make evident', so the patterned actions embody the table which is the theoretical structure to be evidenced.

Nevertheless, this demonstration does have a strong element of the actual and material about it. When the teacher got to the end of the whole thing, and everything had 'happened as it should', he no doubt felt a strong sense of relief. And the class had seen a considerable number of things happening as someone anticipated, lending credence to the feeling that those anticipations might be well founded.

A good deal of what Tom says in the course of the demonstration is directed at the actual, the material, the contingent; at the fact that things do not *have* to turn out quite as expected.

> *Tom:* Make sure you're on that side [*of the safety screen*]. I'll tell you, I'll tell you a story. We had a teacher here a couple of years ago, and some of the sodium we had, this is new stuff by the way, we had some old stuff, and he was given this in a jar, a glass jar, that had been with us for about 10 years, and it had a, a black crust around it, and the stuff had obviously, you know, gone off, and this chap got a piece of that the size of the lump I'm gonna be putting in now, and er, it just blew the jar to pieces.
>
> *Student:* As soon as he put it in?
>
> *Tom:* Coloured, you know, coloured sparks going up here [*makes firework gesture*] and it blew the jar to pieces. It's very very unpredictable, and at other times it'll just go [*makes buzzing sound and a circling gesture with a finger*], around the bath, but I mean, it's very, that's why that's there, [*reaches out and touches the safety screen*] We hope that what – that what you're going to see isn't going to be that reactive, but er, on the other hand–. All right, so, sodium. Ready! [*drops the sodium in the water and steps back quickly*]

Tom capitalizes on the dangerous aspects of the demonstration (which are real enough) to achieve two different things at once. He creates expectations of possible danger and drama, thereby achieving one of the most basic forms of difference (in the sense of Chapter 2) – namely, excitement arising from hope mingled with fear. The students are kept watching in hope of catastrophe. But at the same time, he creates a second difference, creating a different need to explain, out of his knowledge of how to avoid danger. What follows shows his skilful manipulation of these factors, as he moves from lithium to the more reactive sodium.

Tom: Let's have a look at the next one.
Student: Are you going to put that big chunk in?
Tom: No, I'm not, no. This is, again, chemicals are very unpredictable, you've got to be so so careful, it's not, it's not the sort of thing you can, just mess about with. Right, sodium.
Student: Sir, is it expensive, lithium?
Tom: They are, they are fairly expensive, right. Next heading then, Sodium.
Student: Who's book's this?
Tom: A bit like this here would blow the room up actually [*holds a sizeable lump of sodium up before the class, using tweezers*] Ahh, right, what colour is it?
Student: Silver-white.
Tom: It's a silver-white colour when it's oxidized, or tarnished.
Student: Put it all in.
Tom: No I won't. I wouldn't, I wouldn't be here tomorrow if I did. Ahh, nor would you.

The timing of this has interest, too. By choosing this moment – the passage from the least reactive element to the next more reactive one, he builds the tabular comparison of reactivity into the affective as well as the cognitive structure of the demonstration. Tom checks whether they are expecting the sequence to develop, and in doing so communicates that there should be such expectations, that there is a developing structure, by asking for predictions of what may happen when the next element is tried.

Tom: Well, what do you predict? You tell me what you think is going to happen now.
Student: It's going to, catch fire, and
Tom: I'm going to put potassium in there in a minute.
Student: change the colour of the water.
Tom: That's right, so let's, let's get rid of this, and er, get it back to green again. Get some new water.
Student: It'll stay the same colour.
Tom: Okay, so we think it's going to turn the water purple. How about, how about how violently reactive, you think it's going to be more reactive?
Student: Oh yeah.
Tom: How about when I cut it?
Student: Softer, and it's going to be bright inside.

Student: It's going to tarnish very quickly.
Student: Yeah, yeah.
Tom: So you think it's going to be very, it's going to tarnish very very fast, and is going to be soft or harder?
Student: Harder.
Student: Softer.
Students: Softer.

As a result of all this, when he reaches the very reactive potassium, the students are prepared to react strongly, as they see it catching fire spontaneously when dropped in water. Notice Tom's calculated casualness at the start.

Tom: Right then, let's see what happens when we bung this in the water.
Student: Oh god.
[Teacher drops the potassium in the water. It catches fire]
Student: Oh shit.
Student: Did you set it on fire sir?
Student: Does that stuff smell?
Tom: The same gas. Take my word for it, it's the same gas.
[A small explosion]
Student: Shit.
Student: Jeez.
Tom: Right.
[Laughing and giggling]
Tom: Very unpredictable isn't it? . . . the results of previous efforts which you can see on the ceiling there and up there. You see the green splodges on the ceiling?
Student: Oh yeah.
Tom: Okay, that was, that was actually a fairly mild reaction. Erm, so, right then, potassium, burns as, burns as soon as it hits the water, [ ] and then exploded [ ] Yes, it's burned, it's burnt the plastic.
Student: Where?
Tom: There. *[Tom scratches at the safety screen]* That's why it's always a good idea to have a safety screen up.
Student: Burns as soon as it hits the water.

This demonstration then, is at once a conceptual, theoretical event and at the same time has a strong physical *presence*. Its whole structure is dictated by what seems a desiccated and unreal story of elements arranged in numerical order, but that structure is realized – brought into being at the given moment – by a carefully crafted pattern of actions and a well-judged development of emotional tension. These do not merely enliven the event – they exhibit its deep patterning in a way exactly parallel to the underlying theoretical pattern. A bit of the structure of the periodic table has been turned into drama, into something 'made', but also something supported by how things turn out.

Expectation and counterexpectation

Demonstrations – material events pressed in service of theory – may be used to attack or to reshape theoretical expectations. A simple example is the case of making water boil by cooling it. A flask half full of water is boiled until the remainder of the flask is full of water vapour, when it is taken off the flame and sealed. If cold water is run over the outside of the flask, the vapour condenses and the water boils under the reduced pressure. A teacher explains below how and why he uses this demonstration:

> I don't tell them what it's going to be before I start. I ask them to define boiling. You can never tell exactly what they're going to say. In most cases they'll say 'boiling is when you heat up a liquid and you give the particles enough energy to become airborne'... The key is that they associate boiling with heating, and somehow or other I'll get that out of them before we start.

He wants to put in question the common-sense account of boiling, using a phenomenon which seems to defy that account. But just what needs to be explained? Is it, 'How can water boil when the flask is *cooled*?,' or is it, 'If this is "boiling" then what *is* "boiling"?' We incline to think that the real question at issue is the second. The demonstration shows, not so much a surprising effect, as a fracture in understanding. Further advance will be made, not by investigating such phenomena in greater detail or variety, but by a rethinking of explanatory schemes.

The explanation, in terms of vapour pressure in the liquid and in the space above it, will transform what 'boiling' is. After that explanation, the demonstration becomes something different: no longer an unexpected event but now an example of a new theoretical story. It now demonstrates what it previously put in question, namely an account of what boiling is. Not only is knowledge transformed; the demonstration is also transformed.

The teacher above will also tell stories of early expeditions to Mount Everest, where the climbers found it impossible to boil eggs at the high altitude because of the low air pressure, and also of people living a mile above sea level, in Denver, Colorado, needing to use pressure cookers to cook their food. Such anecdotes serve in effect as further demonstrations. A similar function is served by film or videotape of phenomena. For example, the teacher whom we saw explaining about alkali metals promises the class a film of the same experiments with francium.

Tom:	What do you think – how – what do you think rubidium would be like, in terms of its hardness?
Student:	It's soft, really soft.
Tom:	Really very soft, yes. Okay, how about if you put a bit of it in water. Would you want to be in the same room?
Students:	No.
Tom:	No, I wouldn't – no. So this one – francium? It's, I mean the reason we don't do it, one it's violently reactive, two it's incredibly expensive. Er – you'll see a film that we'll show you.

You'll see man with a pipette, and he's got one drip of the stuff, it's actually a very very sort of thick liquid, and he goes like that [*mimes letting a drop fall*] and he runs, and as he runs away you see the jar explode, and er there's this big puff of gas comes out, which is hydrogen, and so it's an extremely violent reaction.

A further example of demonstration being used to transform knowledge is the following, which happens again to concern the meaning of boiling and evaporation. It comes from a Year 9 lesson reviewing phenomena (examples of diffusion) which are to be understood in terms of a molecular theory of matter. This time the demonstration is an experiment recalled in retrospect.

Elaine: Then we looked at the bromine experiment. So, you can actually look at the pictures to remind yourself. The picture on page 54. You put some liquid bromine into the bottom of the gas jar. Bromine is a dark brown colour, and after one hour, what happened to the liquid – the liquid?

Student: It had all gone purple.

Elaine: Yeah, but first of all we had a liquid, it was a liquid in the gas jar. What did the liquid do?

Student: It evaporated.

Elaine: The liquid evaporated, and what does evaporate mean?

Student 1: It turned into a gas.

Student 2: Into a gas.

Elaine: Right, and in evaporating does the liquid boil?

Students: No.

Elaine: So, does a liquid have to boil to evaporate?

Students: No.

Elaine: No, good. The liquid, changed into gas. Why did it change into a gas?

Student: The temperature.

Elaine: Temperature. What does – has temperature got to do with it?

Student: [*Inaudible*]

Elaine: Right, and what were the particles doing when they got hot?

Student: Vibrating.

Student 2: Yeah, they moved faster.

Elaine: They moved faster, good.

Here the teacher is rehearsing a way of making phenomena accountable. That matter happens to diffuse is not the main point. Elaine is doing two things. She is also transforming the notions of 'boiling' and 'evaporating' – here that evaporating need not involve boiling – and she is turning diffusion from an event into an explanatory history. Her explanatory history is one of molecules moving, not one of bromine filling a space. And to do it, 'temperature' has also to have undergone a transformation, from meaning 'feels hotter or colder' to 'is molecules moving faster or slower'. We see again, as in Chapters 3 and 4, the construction of entities and the transformation of knowledge in progress.

What is involved in this last example is not counterexpectation leading to explanation, but explanations used to *create* expectations. The context is one of recalling several parallel demonstrations, all involving diffusion. The idea is clearly to provide them all with a uniform account. The fact that the demonstration is discussed in retrospect, as something to be recalled, suggests how it is not mere brute fact, but that it *stands for something*. It means that molecules move.

Meaning and material action

Throughout this chapter we have been challenging the familiar sharp distinction between words and things, meanings and brute fact, theory and phenomena – 'what we say' and 'what is so'. Our purpose is not at all to suggest that everything is nothing other than just what it is said, or constructed, to be. Our idea is that meanings are closely bound up with the material world and especially with actions on it. Meanings are made from what things can do, what can be done to them, and what they are made of. It is in looking at demonstrations that we can see most clearly how meaning and material action are closely entangled.

The next example concerns not a phenomenon but an instrument. The teacher, Steve, has a microcomputer which can display a graph, and which is connected to a pressure sensor and a temperature sensor. Near the beginning Steve talks to the Year 7 group about the two sensors.

> *Steve*: I've got two things here which can make scientific measurements . . .
> One thing we've got here is a temperature probe. This measures the temperature here [*points at vicinity of probe*], and it's got a little bit of electronic stuff in here [*points inside probe*] and it sends signals along this wire [*gestures along the wire*] into this box and into the computer. So this thing is able to tell the computer how hot this water is . . . This thing [*holds up the second sensor*] is connected to this tube [*holds up tube*]. Now the only thing in the tube is air, so all there is in the tube is air, and the air is connected up to this thing up here which measures pressure.

All the talk is about what things do ('measures the temperature', 'sends signals', 'measures pressure'), and about their parts ('connected to', 'all there is in the tube is air'). What can be done to them is implied (for example, put the temperature probe in the water).

The next thing Steve does is to show, again through action, what 'measuring pressure' means. He connects the pressure sensor to the computer so that its signal will move a cursor up or down on the computer screen.

> *Steve*: . . . if I take this tube out of here, at the moment it's just connected to the air so it's measuring the pressure of air in this room. If I put it in my mouth, it will measure the pressure of the air in my mouth. Now, I'm going to put it in my mouth and I'm going

to blow into the pressure sensor. If I blow into it, the cursor is going to move – the cross in the middle is going to move. Is the cross going to go up or down? Is it going to go left or right?

The students make some guesses, and then Steve tries it.

Steve: Well, let's just, let's just see what happens when I blow into it. Watch the cross. [*Blows into the tube*]
Student: Up.
Steve: And as soon as I stop blowing, it goes down again. So, if the pressure, increases, the cross goes up. Farhan, what's going to happen if I suck? [*Class starts to give answer*]
Steve: No, who's called Fa– put your hand up if your name's Farhan. There's only one Farhan in the class. Farhan, what's going to happen if I suck?
Farhan: Go down.
Steve: It'll go down. Let's just check that out. [*Sucks on the tube*]
Steve: There we go, so when I suck it goes down. So, low pressure is at the bottom, high pressure is at the top.

'Measuring and recording a pressure' is a meaningful, a semiotic event. It is part of communication. And the display screen of the computer is a fully paid-up member of the class of things used to communicate. But it, and the pressure and temperature sensors, is also a material thing whose behaviour is not wholly decided by what we would like it to be. The material and the meaningful are here fully intertwined. What Steve does to explain them is to see what they do and what can be done to them. His actions on the material objects and their responses to those actions become their meaning.

As the lesson proceeds, the material and the meaningful get even closer knit:

Steve: At the moment, the temperature sensor is measuring the temperature of the air in the room. It's just sitting in the air and it's just measuring the temperature of the air. I've got . . . some ice here and a bit of water. So I've got iced water now . . . Omar, do you think? . . . do you understand temperature? Yes? I'm going to put this into the icy water. Do you think it will go down or up? Or do you think it will go right or left? Which way do you think this will go?
Omar: Up.
. . .
Steve: Let's watch what happens when it goes into the cold water [*this is done and everybody watches the screen*]. It's going left, because the temperature scale – on the temperature scale we've got degrees Celsius along the bottom – we've got 0, 50, 100. So – I've just made the temperature quite cold, so it's come back across – it's moved left. Well, it's almost up to the zero line. You see this line here – the line for zero – it's almost got there but not quite.

The cursor goes left or right as the temperature changes, not for any physical reason but for a conventional reason, namely that this was how it was decided to make the display work. It is also a matter of convention to arrange to plot lower values to the left and higher ones to the right. Even assigning the value zero to the temperature of ice and water is conventional. But at the same time, what the class sees is like a material phenomenon: a cross on a screen moves in response to placing a sensor in iced water. What they see differs distinctly from reading a thermometer and plotting a point on a paper graph using a pencil. Communicating and material events are now thoroughly mixed.

Steve then shows how the pressure of air in a tube increases as the temperature of the air is increased. The class are led to note how the points plotted on the screen fall on a rising line. After some time, however, the display suddenly changes all by itself:

Steve: Did you see what the computer did then? I think the computer has decided to swap things around a bit. It's still got all the same readings – it's just changed the scale a little bit.

Now the computer itself has become an actor in these events. Without being asked it changed the scale and so the overall appearance of the plot.

Our point here is that this kind of explanatory episode cannot be understood as meaningful talk about non-meaningful material events. The talk makes meaning out of the events, through actions, and the actions and their material consequences give meaning to the talk. To deal with this kind of data, we are obliged to give up a notion of meaning residing solely in words, in language, and to admit that it emerges from an interplay of language, action and physical events. Where a common-sense view of language says that meaning is carried by words, we have to say that pressure sensors and computers are also objects loaded with meaning. And they get their meaning through actions.

In the above example we have, however, made an easy choice of example. The demonstration was, after all, about an instrument to be used to measure and communicate. The next example, about students understanding sound through action, suggests that making meaning through material action is more general. In this example, the teacher (Leon) has just shown the Year 8 class that none of them can hear sounds of frequency (pitch) higher than about 25 000 oscillations a second. They are looking at data about other animals:

Leon: And how do we know that a dog can hear higher sounds than us? Everybody knows this one. How do we know? . . . Now come on – there – there are some – what do we know about dogs – that people sometimes call them with?

Students: A whistle – whistle – whistle

Leon: And?

Student 1: Whistle

Student 2: They blow the whistle

Student 1: and they
Student 2: and they run
Student 4: It's made a noise but you can't hear it.
Leon: There's a noise but you can't hear it.

What can be done to a dog changes the meaning of 'hearing' ('It's made a noise but you can't hear it'). The teacher later gets the students to sing into a microphone, while others watch the pattern produced on an oscilloscope. This demonstration involves linking the students' own bodies and actions into making new meaning for 'sound'.

Leon: Can you do like a note? When you go 'doh' or something? Or not? ... Can you hold a note?
Student: For long?
Leon: Well go on. Try this.
. . .
Leon: I want you to try
Student: 'Ho-o-o-h'
Leon: to hold a note – see if – see what happens if you are just holding a note. See if we can get that picture up on any note.
Student: 'Ehhhh'
Leon: Like 'Ehhhh'
. . .
Student: 'Ehhhhhh'
Leon: Something like that.
Student: 'Ehhhhhhh'
Leon: Come a bit closer.
Student: 'Ehhhhh' [*Laughter*]
Student 2: Can I have a go?
Leon: It records that laugh, not the note.
. . .
Leon: Hold – hold your note.
Student: 'Ahhhhhhhhhhhhhhhhhhhhh'
Leon: OK, just let me – um [*adjusts oscilloscope*]
Student: That's really good.
Student: Oh that's brilliant.
Leon: That's really good. Now do it again.
Student: 'Ahhhhhhhhhhhhhhhhhhhhhhhhhhhhh'
Leon: Oh, that's brilliant.

There follows work counting the peaks and troughs of the patterns from the sounds students produce and seeing who made the highest frequency sound.

Leon: And was Lois's note high, or lower?
Student: It was higher.
Students: Higher.
Leon: So even with our voices, what makes it high or low?
Student 1: Pitch.
Student 2: Frequency.

Student 3: Frequencies.
Leon: The frequency, the number of vibrations.

Whereas in the example of the properties of alkali metals (see p. 82ff) the students witnessed a demonstration (and from behind a safety screen), here they are an integral part of it. It is *their* actions which are being shown to have new meanings and new possibilities. Their actions produce new effects, and new things are seen to be able to be done to their actions. And in this work, what a student does is treated on a par with what the oscilloscope does, or with what sounds do. All are events being given new meanings.

'What is demonstration, again?'

Apart from our first example, all the other cases of demonstration in this chapter have been actual experiments in the classroom. Our analysis can apply, however, not only to the 'imaginary' demonstration we cited, but to other cases of invoking real events as having theoretical meaning. A prime example of this is the use of narratives about real events. Thus when (Chapter 4, p. 67) the teacher invites recall of food going mouldy, he is doing something very like a demonstration. In the same lesson the teacher (Leon) asked the class to imagine the effect of keeping one half of a cucumber in the fridge for a week, and the other half outside. He again mimed the actions to make the event seem as real as possible. Even more strikingly, the story of Alexis St. Martin's open stomach (previewed in Chapter 2 and given in full in Chapter 7) is, to all intents and purposes, a demonstration in the form of a dramatic tale.

In demonstrations, the material world is made to display and comes to be seen in terms of theoretically meaningful patterns. The material is made into a carrier of meanings. But, in addition, these meanings are always in some sense at risk. The material world can always fail to seem to mean what human beings want to make it mean.

Chapter 6

DYNAMICS OF EXPLANATION

Sources of variation

If at any moment in a lesson we ask the question, 'Why is this explanation being given in this way now?', we get answers which depend on a number of different factors. The factors which generate or constrain explanations are the subject of this chapter. The discussion is organized around four clusters of quite different kinds of influences.

- The first of these draws attention to the fact that explanations occur as part of *explanatory structures*: the way explanations fit alongside and within one another and form a structure reflecting long- and short-term goals.
- The second of these draws attention to the characteristics of *the teacher*: the way explanations are affected by the teacher's personal history, by previous relationships with that class, and by the teacher's stock of explanatory resources.
- The third insists that explanations have to be seen in the context of *the ongoing interaction*: the way explanations belong in a live interactive context, being produced, modified and adjusted in relation to the perceived needs of the moment.
- The fourth points to the influence of *the subject matter*: the way explanations depend on the kind of content being explained, including visible and invisible phenomena, theoretical terms and entities, procedures, and formal devices such as graphs.

We will now consider these four clusterings of influence in turn.

Explanatory structures

We suggested in Chapter 1 that explanations need to be thought of as fitting into a larger explanatory structure. Any given instance of an explanation may contain, and may be contained in, another explanation. Explanatory structures have recognizable shape due to the effects of the three other clusterings of influence. Here we have given them names which point to an organizing principle.

'Guess what teacher's thinking'

We start with five 'snapshot' extracts in sequence from one Year 8 lesson. The subject is 'The Earth in Space'. The teacher is Alan. Our question is: 'What accounts for this sequence of explanations all being part of one lesson, even taking the subject of the lesson as given?'

The five extracts deal, in order, with: planets in the solar system (Extract 1); the speed of light (Extract 2); freezing and evaporation of water (Extract 3); Alan warily deflecting the class from what they want to talk about (Extract 4); gravity (Extract 5). Given this variety, we can ask our question again, more from the teacher's perspective this time: what accounts for these being the things that Alan wants the class to focus on? What is the unifying scheme here?

Extract 1

    Alan: What do you call the collection of the planets that move around our Sun?

    Student: [*inaudible*]

    Alan: You've got Mercury, Venus, Jupiter, Mars, Neptune, Pluto, Uranus . . . all the others. What do you call [?] You didn't put your hand up. Is that what you were going to say? Yes?

    Student: Solar system.

    Alan: Yes, the solar system. OK? So the collection of all of the planets that orbit around the Sun are referred to as the solar system. What is our Sun? Yes?

    Student: Big ball of – er – gas.

    Alan: OK. A big ball of gases. Good. OK.

Extract 2

    Alan: . . . can you remember why we said you sometimes see lightning, and then a little bit later we hear the thunder? What was the reason for that, again? Yes?

    Student: Light travels faster than sound.

    Alan: Because light travels much faster than sound. Can anybody just off the top of their head remember just how fast light travels?

Extract 3

Alan: Let's imagine that we could survive on Mercury, and you were
           trying to drink some water. Just imagine that you perhaps had
           a very special suit on that allowed you to stand there without
           burning up, OK? But you opened your flask or whatever and
           poured some water out. What would happen to the water?

Student: Evaporate.

Alan: It would evaporate straight away. Now then . . . let's imagine we
           were out on Pluto, and again we had a bottle of water.

Student: It would freeze over.

Alan: It would freeze solid. Even if you could get the lid off and tip
           it upside down nothing would come out of it. It would be ice,
           wouldn't it? OK. What is essential for life on Earth? What do we
           all need?

Student: Air.

Alan: Yes.

Student: We need warmth.

Alan: OK, I'm after something in connection with what I've just been
           saying. Can we think of something that we need in order to
           live, in connection with what I was just talking about? Yes?

Student: Water.

Alan: Water OK. As I say we need other things but we need water.

Extract 4

Three students ask Alan if the lesson will include some things they are
interested in. The answers they get are:

Alan: We could certainly mention them and bring them in at some
        stage.

Alan: Right, if we have time that might be quite an interesting thing to
        touch on at some stage.

Alan: Can we come back to a few of those points in a moment?

Extract 5

Alan: Why do the planets keep going round the Sun? Are they joined
           onto the Sun

Student: No.

Alan: –in any way? So what actually keeps them going round? Why
           don't they just go off by themselves? Why do they stay in those
           nice little orbits?

. . .

Alan: The planets keep on spinning round the Sun because they're
           held in place by something called 'gravity'.

The answer it turns out, is simple. Alan has a plan: it is to set an exercise on
a table in the students' textbook which gives the distances of planets from

the Sun, their times to orbit the Sun, their diameters and their surface temperatures. He is directing the lesson to provide ways of relating these quantities to one another. It is the data in the table – yet to be seen by the class – which direct decisions about which questions, answers and explanations will be treated as relevant. Given the role of the Sun as a hot star, surface temperatures of the planets can be related to their distances from the Sun. Their orbital periods also relate to these distances. The absolute scale of the solar system (e.g. eight light-minutes from the Sun to the Earth) can also be appreciated.

Alan's insistence on water, as opposed to other things needed for life (Extract 3), is related to the fact that the table contains temperatures from which one can infer the state of water on a given planet, and so something about the possibility of life as it exists on Earth. The seemingly odd sequence of Extract 3, in which the state of water on Mercury and Pluto is first discussed, followed by questions about living things' need for water, now makes sense because this is the sequence of thought working from the table as something given. In Extract 2, Alan hints at how one could read the scale of the solar system from the table. In Extract 5 he suggests how to think about the orbiting of the planets.

Alan's agenda explains his choice of topics, and why it is always he who chooses the topic. He insists on one answer where another would do: 'Can we think of something . . . in connection with what I was just talking about?' The price is that the choice of topics, their sequence, and the explanatory structure itself may seem arbitrary to the students in the class. They do not yet have access to Alan's plan.

Some would be critical of this teacher's approach. But that is not here our point. The point is that what explanations are offered and what is treated as relevant are always functions of a larger structure, in this case the demands of a task which is to come.

'Sophie's question'

Our second example shows how the characteristics of a single brief explanatory moment in a lesson need to be accounted for by the much larger explanatory structure within which it fits. In this case, however, it is a structure extending over a whole series of lessons. The example comes from the series of Year 10 lessons on the periodic table given by Ruth, mentioned in Chapter 4. Ruth is explaining how, given the total number of electrons in an atom of an element, one assigns different numbers of them to successive 'completed' or 'full' 'shells', ending with some number in the outermost 'shell'. This last number plays a crucial role in deciding the chemical properties of the element, groups of elements with the same number of electrons in the outer 'shell' having a family resemblance in their properties. The groups are labelled with this number (e.g. Group I elements have atoms with one electron in the outermost shell). Thus from pure counting one can predict some chemical behaviour. The extract starts with Ruth summarizing what has been said so far.

Ruth: So you've got two electrons in the first shell. Most of you have got it down already. Eight in the second shell. Eight or eighteen in the third shell. Eighteen in the fourth shell, and thirty-two in the fifth shell.

Sophie: Miss, how do you know when to use eight or eighteen?

Ruth: I'll go over that when we come back to what we're doing today. I did it on the board for you earlier on, if you remember, last week.

Sophie: I know, but I've forgotten.

Ruth: You've forgotten, have you? I'll come back to that question. I'll definitely come back to it.

. . . [*A few minutes later*]

Ruth: Right, I'm going over Sophie's question, and then after I've done Sophie's question I'm going to do the periodic table. Right, Sophie was asking, 'How do you know, whether to use eight or eighteen'. Who's going to tell her?

Student: It depends on what the number is.

Ruth: On the group number. Right, so we'll take sodium, Na. How many electrons has sodium got?

. . .

[*Ruth establishes from the periodic table that sodium has eleven electrons, which can be placed two, eight and one in successive shells. She then takes other cases where again there is only one answer. Then she takes the example of bromine, in Group VII with 35 electrons, and gets the class to produce two patterns of numbers of electrons. Only one pattern has seven in the final shell*]

. . .

Ruth: That's ten, and eighteen gives you twenty eight and seven gives you thirty-five. But if you used eight there, it would be ten, eighteen, and what number would you need to make thirty-five?

Student: Seventeen.

Ruth: Seventeen.

Ruth: Right. So the last number has to be seven. For Group VII. So this arrangement is correct. [*Ticks the first list of numbers*] And out of these two which arrangement would you use?

Student: The top one.

Ruth: Right. So you use eight or eighteen in the circle, so that the last number, is the same as the group number. Is that okay Sophie?

Student: Yeah. [*Confidently*]

Ruth: Would you like to explain it to me?

Sophie: Yeah. The number at the end has to be the same as the group number.

Ruth makes an interesting about-turn in her explanation, prompted by Sophie's question. The idea of this counting game is that chemical family properties can be predicted from counting electrons. The explanation turns this around to use knowledge of the group number, and so of the family properties, to find the right way to count electrons so as to place an atom in the correct group. Sophie is told to use knowledge of what should be predicted to decide how to make the prediction. Why does this happen? The answer is to be found in the large-scale explanatory context. Ruth has made, consistently and from the start, a definite choice of how to explain the periodic table. This choice is one of the possible didactic transformations which can be made, and which we analysed in Chapter 4. Instead of discussing the periodic table as a pattern of chemical properties, explained by patterns of electrons in shells, Ruth (perhaps judging that her class does not know enough about properties of chemical elements) offers the periodic table as a given scheme for predicting these properties.

In these lessons, therefore, the periodic table is presented as a *given representation*, from which one can work out aspects of the behaviour of reality. The representation comes first, and reality second. The representation is justified, not as a summary of what elements are like, but as based on a scheme of numbers of electrons 'filling shells'. Unfortunately, this scheme, more fully explained, is subtler than Ruth wants to admit. By a quirk of the values of energies of electrons in atoms in the presence of electrons already there, the third shell may be left 'partly complete' with eight electrons or fully complete with eighteen. Since it seems too difficult to explain this to this class, she is obliged to reverse the logic of the explanation: instead of counting correctly to predict chemical properties, you use chemical properties to decide how to count correctly.

Against this background, what can we say about the explanatory context? Sophie wants to know, and Ruth wants to teach her, how to get the right answer to an examination question of the form, 'What is the electron configuration of element X?' The scientific story behind that question is long and complex. Given the contingencies of the pedagogic environment, Ruth cannot (nor could any teacher) tell the whole story. Instead, the knowledge it represents has had to be transformed into another form. Mendeleev's table, with additions from which one can read off numbers of electrons, comes to occupy pride of place. It is used as a representation, to be taken as given, from which to *read off* chemistry. This makes it possible for Ruth to make claims about the simplicity and logic of chemistry ('It really does help you understand chemistry'). But it leaves Ruth – and other teachers like her – with the difficulty that the basis of the representation cannot be properly explained. That basis comes out as a story about 'filling shells'. This is where Ruth used the analogy of filling chairs in rows, discussed in Chapter 4.

'You can't exactly magic it in'

In the first example above, there were issues arising from a plan hidden, initially, from the class. This plan decided what would be proper answers to be rehearsed before the questions got asked. In the second example the existence of answers shaped what questions had to be constructed. In our next example, the explanatory structure is organized by a topic to be thought about, in which it becomes one of the teacher's tasks to respond to common-sense challenges from students.

The teacher, Leon, and his Year 7 class have been talking about microbes rapidly increasing in number.

Student: **How does a microbe reproduce? It can't just say, 'I'll have another one'. How do they do that?**

Leon: It's a good question, because we reproduce. We sort of go – you know, we go wherever you go – the (disco?) or something – 'Oh, I'll have that one'. This is what we do. You pick one, yes? – and you usually get married or whatever with somebody. We do that – we choose, right? Now the choice is either microbes have sort of like little male and female ones – are there? Could they? Could you get male and female and stuff? I suppose there's no problem, but microbes do actually – Nina, strangely enough – I know it sounds incredible – actually do what you said. It sounds amazing, but just take it in – right? – they don't go to the Palais – this is what they do – it's amazing this – what I'm going to say to you – right? – You have one microbe could land on a piece of (food) – literally one microbe lands on a piece of food – it now starts to feed on and digest that food and starts to grow – yeah? – so it gets larger – not massively like but it's feeding and growing, right? OK, it's bigger now than it was before, OK? What the microbe can actually do

Student: It mates with itself.

Leon: no it doesn't mate with itself, all it does is it splits in two.

Student: Like an egg.

Leon: Like an egg shell . . . with what?

Student: [*Inaudible*]

Leon: Yes?

Student: If you've got one microbe –

Leon: If you go back with microbes and stuff far enough there must have been at the beginning – right? – where this little organism – right? – sort of developed and was able to make copies of itself, and that's where it started. It was just able to make copies of itself.

Student: How does that [ ] whatever made it that first [ ]?

Leon: Get started?

Student: Yes. **Because you can't exactly magic it in**

Leon: No, you can't magic it. There are chemicals – OK? – just try to get this, it's hard to sort of picture in your head. But there are chemicals – yeah? – I mean just one side of . . . not the other side, but you know the bits that made up the . . . the little bits . . . the little . . . imagine you had lots of them just lying around, right? Now what could you do with the little bits if you had one side of the (molecule?). What could you do with these little odd pieces?

Student: Attach them to –

Leon: You could click them in – yeah? – you could click them in –
            yeah – so now you've got almost like a proper (molecule?). If
            you could join all those little . . . now they're in a row if you
            join them up – you could pull the two apart and what have you
            got now?

Student: Two halves.

Leon: Two halves. Now if you've got more of these little bits around
            what could you now do?

Student: Make a bigger one.

Leon: Start all over again. So if you started off with one, and you're
            able to make a copy what can you do now? Make a copy from
            both of them.

Student: And make a copy.

Leon: And you could keep on going on and on, yeah? So you see what
            I'm saying is, if you could get some chemicals that could copy
            themselves and could eventually end up with a – like a microbe.

Student: ***I've got a question. You know microbes attack – you
            know like . . . Do they go to the toilet?***

In contrast with Alan and Ruth, we see Leon willing to construct, off the
cuff, explanations of things in which he has aroused interest: asexual reproduction and cell division, and of the origin of life in replicating molecules.
The pattern continues: the last question ('Do they go to the toilet?') gets
Leon to explain how the poisonous waste products of microbes can cause
illnesses.

This explanatory context, shaped by the students' interests and encouraged by the teacher's behaviour, produces a number of demands on the
teacher. There has to be a recognition of what it is the student may be
asking. There has to be a continual process of adapting the explanation
to the audience – very evident in the frequent pausing and checking. And
there has to be a stock of background knowledge, both the students' and
the teacher's, ready to be drawn upon, and able to be transformed in real
time into forms which make sense to the audience.

The matters to be explained can be unpredictable. Leon could not have
known that the very profound issue, 'You can't exactly magic it in', was
going to be raised.

Just because of these features, it is in explanatory contexts of the kind
exemplified here that we most often see what one might have supposed
to be the normal form of explanation: a 'how' or 'why' question followed
by an account directed to that question. Yet more often than not we see
complex interlocking patterns of explanation produced not so much by re-
quests for explanations as by the need to produce explanations within some
previously worked out framework. Does this mean that Leon's classroom
proves an exception to our assumption about explanatory structures? We
think not. An oversimplified comparison suggests that in Alan's classroom
the structure of a pregiven object (e.g. a section of a textbook) organizes the

explanatory sequence. In Ruth's case a canonical representation, the periodic table, is used to organize explanatory structures. In Leon's case, the guiding principle is his assumptions about the relations between scientific and everyday, common-sense knowledge. In each of these cases, what may appear as teacher style and differences in pedagogic strategies rest on underlying organizing principles tightly related to conceptions of science.

We move now to consider the second 'clustering of influences', in the shape of the teacher.

The teacher

Science teachers have, as a result of their professional experience, a variety of ways of explaining things at appropriate levels. An experienced teacher will be able to switch at a moment's notice into an explanation of electric circuits, of respiration, or of combustion, suited to (say) 14 year-olds or to A-level. Thus it is that we rather rarely see explanations newly minted in the classroom. For the most part, we see fairly well-practised explanations – explanations whose characteristics would come as no surprise to other science teachers. Yet all the time, new explanatory resources are also being developed and shared amongst teachers, and are being tried out. That this is what is (or was going to be) what happened in the following extract is visible largely because the intended resource was not in fact available at the time. The class is from Year 8.

> *Alan*:   I want to try and get across to you this morning just how large everything out there is – how absolutely phenomenally large things are. OK? I'm going to start the [ ] there is a book somewhere which we actually have in school which I was trying to get hold of this morning without any success – and it starts off [ ]virtually looking at molecules
>   . . .
>   It then shows a person standing in the middle of a field, OK? Then it shows a photograph of that person that's taken from an aeroplane so that the person appears to be quite small – you can begin to get some idea of the size of the Earth – and then those photographs which are taken of the Earth by satellite OK? So you just see a little circle of the Earth down there and it gets further and further away until it gets right out of the solar system.
>
> *Student*: We've got a picture of that in our maths class.
>
> *Alan*:   Have you? Right. So you've seen something on those lines before. Er – I think it's called something like 'On a scale of ten'* or something, because every picture is ten times bigger than the previous picture. I'll see if I can get it for you.

* Alan is referring to a book, *Powers of Ten* by Philip and Phylis Morrison, W.H. Freeman.

How a teacher explains also has a personal history of previous attempts at explaining with a variety of classes, experiencing what seems to work and what seems not to work. Alan knows of a potentially valuable resource, which he does not have to hand. His difficulty arises from the attempt to describe, in language, information which is presented visually.

More often, explanations follow well-rehearsed paths, with the teacher using ways of explaining that have previously worked well. An example might be the following account of the formation of fossil fuels with a Year 7 group.

Elaine: OK. Burning fossil fuels and wood puts carbon dioxide into the atmosphere.
Student: Can we [*inaudible*]?
Elaine: In a minute. How do – how are fossil fuels actually produced?
Student: Over millions of years.
Elaine: Over millions and millions of years. From what?
Student: Dead animals.
Elaine: Right, dead animals and plants. What happens to them?
Student: They rot.
Elaine: They rot. Where do they disintegrate, do they rot?
Student: Under the ground.
Elaine: Under the ground. OK. Which sort of bacteria are we talking about probably?
Student: Oxygen [ ] nitrogen?
Elaine: Oxygen-hating bacteria. OK. So the animals when they die, over millions of years, turn into [?]
Student: Fossils.
Elaine: Fossil fuels. And then when we burn them, we release energy and we release carbon dioxide.

Elaine has made a number of distinctive choices, for example not to distinguish types of fossil fuel such as petroleum or coal and so not to distinguish plant or animal origins. For her present purpose, the broad picture may be enough. This emphasis on the recognizability and 'normality' of many explanations must not be taken too far. Like many teachers, Elaine can improvise around a fixed theme, using material that comes from the class or that she thinks of on the spur of the moment. An example comes from work on the same topic, but with Year 9.

Elaine: We're adding to the carbon dioxide in the air every time we breathe out. Something is going on in our bodies that's making carbon dioxide? Mary?
Mary: Food.
Elaine: It's something to do with food.
Student: [*Inaudible*]
Elaine: Good.
Student: Photosynthesis.
Elaine: That's what the plants do.

[*Student laughter*]

Elaine: Now, it's not funny, that

Student: Respiration.

Elaine: hey, good, it's not as funny as you think. What's the connection between respiration and photosynthesis?

Student: They go together.

Elaine: How do they go together?

Instead of rejecting the reply 'photosynthesis' as wrong or inappropriate, Elaine uses it to shift to a more general level of explanation. In this lesson she next explains how photosynthesis traps carbon from carbon dioxide in the atmosphere, which becomes incorporated in food for animals, and is released through respiration. She might have gone even deeper, pointing out that each process is very much like the other in reverse. Thus, in responding to a question and then to a mistake, she improvises a deeper explanation than she may have at first intended. Elaine also seems to be improvising in the following, a little later in the same lesson.

Elaine: The oxygen I just breathed in is probably still going round in my blood stream, and the carbon dioxide I'm breathing out is from some oxygen I breathed in a little while ago. Right, OK, so the animals breathe out carbon dioxide during the process that we call res [?]

Student: Respiration.

Elaine: Respiration, good. And that's the process where we release energy from the food that we've eaten, by breathing in the oxygen. The oxygen goes all round our bodies in the blood stream. Gets to every little part of us, every cell, every brain cell, every cell in my big toe down to my finger tips, round to my back, up to my shoulders. The oxygen goes all round to every cell and reacts with the food that I've digested to release energy.

Elaine's rather vivid evocation of how oxygen 'gets to every little part of us' suggests a teacher with a substantial set of explanatory resources, drawing on them in a flexible and varied way according to what she judges to be the needs of the occasion. Like the virtuoso cadenzas in a concerto, such explanations are simultaneously improvised and practised.

The teacher's relationship with the class

We mentioned earlier the interrelation of the teacher's pedagogic strategies and style, and the characteristics of explanatory structures. That left the picture too one-sided. On the one hand, it suggests that teachers have a pedagogic style – as we are attempting to show, strategies and styles are a result of histories of experience. On the other hand, there is an implied assumption that 'classes' are inherently different, so that what happens in Alan's, Ruth's, and Leon's classrooms points to differently disposed collections of students.

The reality is more likely that Leon's strategy, as much as Ruth's and Alan's, make possible, foster, encourage, allow the students to develop particular forms of interaction. It needs a relatively close look at microstructures of interaction to get at this. Take the example of how each teacher deals with questions. In Leon's classroom students can initiate discourse:

Student: How does a microbe reproduce? It can't just say, 'I'll have another one'. How do they do that?
Leon: It's a good question . . .

Student: How does that [ ] whatever made it that first [ ]?
Leon: Get started?
Student: Yes. Because you can't exactly magic it in.
Leon: No, you can't magic it.

Questions are initiated by students; they are not just admitted, they are 'taken up' seriously, and taken as part of a dialogue; so, for instance, the student's, 'Because you can't exactly magic it in', is not just a statement (rather than a question), it is a very confidently and challengingly made statement. Clearly, the members of a class will respond in particular ways to this mode.

In Ruth's class the strategies are different. Students also initiate questions:

Sophie: Miss, how do you know when to use eight or eighteen?
Ruth: ·I'll go over that when we come back to what we're doing today. I did it on the board for you earlier on, if you remember, last week.
Sophie: I know, but I've forgotten.
Ruth: You've forgotten, have you? I'll come back to that question. I'll definitely come back to it.

Here the teacher's strategy is to defer answering until the 'proper place' in the explanation is reached. Whereas in Leon's classroom students are involved in the developing organization of the sequence, here they are not. Here, student questions, when they are answered, are answered in terms of providing content within the structure.

In Alan's classroom students tend not to initiate questions. Their answers are quite closely circumscribed by the demands of the schema which their teacher has in mind; his questions tend to have the function of making students the 'sayers' of already established content; thus, perhaps making that knowledge theirs, or securing their participation in the sequence:

Alan: What is our Sun? Yes?
Student: Big ball of – er – gas.
Alan: OK. A big ball of gases. Good. OK.

As we saw, responses to student initiated questions look like this:

Alan: Right, if we have time that might be quite an interesting thing to touch on at some stage.

Broadly speaking, a strongly framed, pre-existing explanatory sequence keeps student questions at bay.

In general, this aspect of classroom interaction throws light not only on the generation of different kinds of explanatory sequences, but on a teacher's epistemological stance, on aspects of their personal and social dispositions, and importantly for our focus, it allows us an insight into what a teacher thinks an explanation is and is meant to do. With this we come to consider our third clustering of influences, the ongoing interaction.

The ongoing interaction

In this section we look at what, in the dynamic interaction of the classroom, leads to particular explanatory resources being chosen, especially the effect of immediate feedback which students produce as a lesson evolves. This means looking at how the teacher's behaviour depends on what students do. It also means looking at how students are constrained by the strategies used by the teacher.

It is rare to see examples of 'complete explanation first time around'. Very often, explanations are conducted by some form of question and answer, with the teacher correcting, rewording and adding to answers to fill out a more complete and correct account. That is, many explanations in the science classroom have the nature of rehearsal, of going over partial explanations given previously and elaborating and correcting them. Explanations often seem to be established by repetition rather than by attempting to present them once and for all.

Explanations are thus often constructed in interaction with the class, attempting to draw out what they know, and to incorporate this in an explanation. The nature of the ongoing interaction is then crucial for the way explanations turn out, and is something the teacher has at the same time to stimulate or provoke and to control and manipulate.

During the course of a lesson, the nature of the job in hand changes continuously. There may be a brief aside – it may be explaining a word. The lesson may have phases when pupils produce ideas, and other phases when the teacher does something with those ideas. Other tasks include: opening up a new issue; clarifying a point; crystallizing an issue; giving new information; eliciting pupils' ideas; correcting a misapprehension; getting pupils to think something through, and so on. All affect how explaining is done, and the kind of explanation which is needed will depend on the kind of interaction the teacher encourages and can manage. In this section we describe some of them.

Problem for some, explanation for all

Students don't necessarily say if they have problems or doubts – and sometimes they can't. The teacher has then to look for signals and to provoke feedback. This may involve direct questioning, but also involves subtler ways of reading students' behaviour in the light of one's knowledge of them. In Chapter 2, we described a teacher – Steve – finding a student who thought that the melted wax was water (a not uncommon idea). Here is how Steve begins to get his Year 7 class as a whole to hear what each other thinks has happened.

Steve: It melted into water? So, Daniel, have you got, in your tube at the moment, have you got some wak–, have you got some water?

Daniel: Yes, sir.

Steve: There's water in the tube, says Daniel. Put your hand up if you agree with Daniel that there is some water in the tube.

Student: No.

Steve: Now, if you agree with Daniel that there is water in the tube, put your hand up. Okay, so some people think there may be water in the tube. Kersuma, why do you think that there's water in the tube?

Kersuma: I don't think so.

Steve: You don't think there's water in the tube. Okay, right, why do you think Daniel thinks that there is water in the tube?

Kersuma: Because it looks like water.

This discussion of what is in the tube opens up a space for anybody who might agree with Daniel that melted wax is water to join in, and Steve creates a chance to explain not merely that an idea is wrong, but that there may be a good reason why people get it wrong. Feedback from one student has been converted into explanatory feedback for all.

Terms and meanings

In the same lesson Steve talks to a small group about how they would describe 'the stuff inside the test tube'. They use the rather vivid and well-motivated term 'see-through', a meaning directly linked to action. Steve would like them to replace it by 'transparent'. Steve's justification for preferring one term to the other is that 'transparent' is 'scientific' – which of course it is by custom, not by merit.

Steve: In what ways is it similar to water?

Student: It's see-through.

Steve: It's see-through. What's another word for see-through? Another word for see-through. We want a scientific word for see-through? . . . we'll come up with it later . . . Apart from being see-through, what about its, has it got the same colour as water?

Student: Yes.

Steve: What colour's that? Has it got a colour?

Student: No.

Steve: So it's colour [?]

Student: It's clear.

Steve: It's clear, oh, well clear could mean see-through, couldn't it, yeah? Lucozade's clear, but it's got a colour. Yeah? So what's this, has it got a colour?

Student: No.

Steve: So, it's colour [?] colour [?] Colourless. It's colourless.

Student: [*Inaudible*]

Steve: It's colourless. It's colourless and see-through. It's transparent. That's a word for see-through.

We remarked in discussing metaphor in Chapter 4 that the Latin root of transparent is *trans parare*, that is, 'appear through'. Transparent is indeed 'a word for see-through'. Later on this is recapitulated to the class as a whole and they start using the newly learned words in different cases. This process of rehearsal implicitly explains, through use, when and in what contexts these words should be used.

Telling what we'll do by asking what you know

In Chapter 2 we looked at signalling the nature of a new topic. One way to do so is to ask questions. The questions may also serve as an 'on-line' assessment of where it is best to start, so that explanations are tuned to what students know already. In our next example, Ruth revises ideas from Year 9 on particles before introducing the periodic table to a Year 10 class. She has an idea of how she wants to introduce the table but she needs to make sure it is going to work.

Ruth: Now in Year 9 you did a small amount of work on particles now I want to expand your ideas. What are the names of the particles that you know about?

Student: Atoms.

Ruth: Atoms and at the beginning of the course in Year 10 we said that atoms were made of three specific [?]

Student: [*Inaudible*]

Ruth: Protons electrons and [?]

Student: Neutrons.

Ruth: Neutrons. And are all atoms different?

Student: [*A few*] Yes.

Ruth: Why are they different?

Student: [*Inaudible*]

Ruth: They have different numbers of those particles. Do you know why they have different numbers of those particles? Do you know what's different about groups?

Student: [*Inaudible*]

Ruth: They've got different elements of . . . particles and . . . different elements. And what table can you tell the number from?

Students: [*A few*] periodic table.

Ruth: Periodic table.

Such exchanges tell the class that they will be working on the periodic table, and that protons, electrons and neutrons will be involved. And they tell Ruth where she has to start.

Collecting and using ideas

Teachers often set themselves the goal of weaving explanations out of ideas and contributions from the class, and furthermore to give most students a chance of contributing. This is not necessarily easy. In the following extract from a Year 7 lesson, Leon has to get students to listen carefully to each other:

Nina: I wrote 'microbes are possibly the smallest, possibly, the smallest cells, cells I think, which you can only see through a microscope'.

Leon: Alright who agrees with that? Who agrees that you need a microscope to see them?

Students: Yeah.

. . .

Leon: OK so but we did say an interess–, you did say an important thing about them, we just said they're living things. What did she say that was extra to that?

Sally: They live in human bodies.

Leon: No, she didn't, Sally. Say it again and see if you can spot it. Listen.

Nina: Microbes are something that are lit–, tiny living cells in the human body.

Leon: Did you spot it?

Sally: Cells.

Leon selects part of what Nina wrote about microbes ('that you can only see microbes through a microscope') and follows that up with the rest of the class. However, she has also mentioned other relevant information ('that they are small cells') which he must not forget to address. Many explanations require a complex of ideas to be collected. By listening not just to the ways contributions are phrased but also by paying attention to what is missing, the teacher can get an indication of which points need to be reinforced or which may not have been properly understood.

An insistence on involving students in at least the partial production of explanations obviously leads to trouble if they do not know enough of what the teacher wants them to contribute. In such cases teachers often resort to verbal or intonational clues, for example leaving words unfinished, leaving sentences incomplete but with strong structural hints as to the required filler, and by playing with stress and intonation. We saw an example earlier in this chapter:

Elaine: So the animals when they die, over millions of years, turn into [?]

Student: Fossils.
Elaine: Fossil fuels.

With this we now come to discuss the fourth of our clusterings of interest, the influence of the subject matter to be explained.

The subject matter to be explained

What kind of explanation is needed obviously depends on what is to be explained. Explaining how joints in the skeleton work needs nothing that cannot in principle be seen or touched, but explaining evaporation involves the invisible and intangible motion of molecules. Explaining the meaning of the display of a sound on a cathode ray oscilloscope involves explaining both the invisible action of a sound wave and the conventional and artificial form of its display as a graph. Explaining how to do something is not the same as explaining a phenomenon. Both differ from explaining terms and conventions.

We do not, however, find pure cases of forms of explanation for different kinds of thing to be explained. Conventions are rarely if ever pure conventions, but are motivated by an understanding of how things are. An account of how something works is often accompanied by introducing new terms which help to organize and frame the account. How to do something depends on how things work and what they are.

We will give one example here and then briefly indicate others to be found elsewhere in the book. The example here is about explaining inherently intangible things.

Explaining the intangible

Is a magnetic field something real? Or is it just a way of talking about places where magnetic effects occur? Michael Faraday was clear that this is a real question:

> I have recently been engaged in describing and defining the lines of magnetic force ... I am now about to leave the strict line of reasoning for a time, and enter upon a few speculations respecting the physical character of the lines of force ...
>
> (Michael Faraday, *Experimental Researches*: para 3243)

Faraday went on to speculate that magnetic fields were as real as any material substance. At the time, a substantial body of opinion held the opposite view: that magnetic fields are a mathematical fiction. Pupils have an analogous difficulty; what they hear called 'a magnetic field' looks remarkably like empty space. To be sure, curious things happen in that space, but does that mean that there is anything curious *in* that space? In the lesson discussed below, the teacher (Alan) puts considerable effort into making magnetic fields real and substantial for his Year 7 class. He does it both in the way he talks, through the way he acts, and through the examples he brings into focus. Here are all three at work, in a discussion which follows Alan having reminded the class that he previously got them to feel how hard it was to pull a piece of iron off of a large magnet:

Alan: Now then, I don't suppose this is the sort of place that you'd go and hang out at weekends, but how many of you have been to scrap yards before? You may have seen as cars – as the old crushed cars are being moved around the scrap yard

Student: Oh yeah – that big – like that big round magnet – it goes and drops on the thing and then it's crushed into a square [*student gestures a large round object in mid air*]

Alan: OK, brilliant. Some of the scrap yards have on the bottom of their cranes a great big magnet [*Alan holds his hands out wide*]. So all the crane driver does, is move the magnet over the top of a car, lowers it and the car goes 'boing', sticks to the magnet, and they can lift the magnet up on the end of the crane and up comes the car as well, stuck to the magnet [*Alan mimes all this with vertical movements of his two hands*]. And then they can move it across – if it's going in one of those crushers – those car crushers [*crushing gesture*]. Brilliant. If this magnet is strong enough to lift a car, do you imagine that you have half a dozen people going like that [*Alan braces a foot against a table and mimes a struggle to pull something towards him*] trying to pull the car back off the magnet when they've finished?

One thing Alan is doing is opening up the possibility that it must be possible to switch magnets on and off (the lesson is about electromagnets). But another thing he is doing, through the very concrete and physical character of the talk, through his bodily gesture, and through the choice of example of lifting something very heavy, is to suggest the real physicality of magnetic effects. 'What's big and strong must be real,' goes the rhetoric. Alan then reminds the class of practical work they have just done looking at magnetic fields visualized using iron filings:

Alan: One or two of you got as far as sprinkling iron filings over a sheet of paper under which there was a bar magnet. OK, what did you see if you did that?

Student: There was a – the iron filings – some of them – stuck to the bar magnet and you saw the shape of the bar magnet, and they like made circle patterns round the outside.

Alan: OK brilliant, so in other words a little bit like this pattern up here [*points to a photograph of filing patterns in a book he holds up*].

The curved nature of the filing patterns was salient for the student. For Faraday, that was reason enough to think the field real:

It appears to me, that the outer forces at the poles can only have relation to one another by *curved* lines of force through the surrounding space;

and I cannot conceive curved lines of force without the conditions of physical existence in that intermediate space.

(Michael Faraday, *Experimental Researches*: para 3258)

A part of Alan's lesson is given over to looking at photographs of these patterns, implicitly evoking fields as being 'out there'. Alan is plainly conscious that what he is on about involves a concern for the material existence of fields:

> *Alan*: You can't see these magnetic field lines, but if you hold two magnets together, you can tell those magnetic field lines must be there, because if you have two poles the same they interact and try to push each other apart, don't they? [*Gestures hands pushed together and then apart*]. . . . so you can tell there is something there in that space but you can't see it. However, if you sprinkle iron filings over a magnet the iron filings stick to the points where the magnetic field is – where the magnetic field lines are. And that enables you to see them, OK?

Alan's language presupposes that magnetic fields have material existence, and appeals to the 'Doubting Thomas' in students, making touch the touchstone of the real. So interested is he in using the visual effect of iron filings patterns to add to this sense of reality, that he offers a less than reputable account of how filings reveal field shapes; an account that presumes that the field lines are something 'there' to which iron filings can 'stick'. Notice also how 'magnetic field lines' have started to appear in Alan's story as unseen agents able to act. A little later, talking about the Earth's magnetic field, field lines start to play the active agent role in clauses, both for Alan and for the student who answers him:

> *Alan*: Can you remember we were saying that if you were standing directly over the magnetic north or the magnetic south your mag– your compass would behave rather strangely? OK, can you see why that is, in relation to field lines? To what the field lines do at the poles? Yes?
>
> *Student*: When they reach the pole they start to stick up, don't they?

Magnetic fields are in process of being transformed, for these students, from empty space where something happens, to a something present which acts of its own accord. The explanatory issue here is very plainly the construction of a new entity, and Alan's work through language, his body, his focus on impressive powers and his choice of activities real and imagined for the class, all work together to this end. Without his telling them to, the students themselves begin to use his way of talking.

Other examples

Another example in which the nature of the subject matter calls for explanations to involve a lot of theoretical imagination is to be found at the end of Chapter 7, in a lesson on the movement of the continents. There the issue is, rather than intangibility, the remoteness from any possible experience of what is being used in the explanation. As in the case of magnetic fields above, the teacher there uses a large amount of gesture and body language to evoke the events his explanation requires.

A rather different pair of examples is that of teaching density (Chapter 3) and teaching graphs using a computer (Chapter 5). In both these cases, much of the work goes into making abstractions – and in the case of graphs, conventions too – seem very concrete.

Finally, earlier in this chapter and also in Chapter 4, we discussed work on the chemical periodic table. This subject matter is a grand classification scheme, which demands a rather complex approach to explanation. Is it to be treated as an extensive classification of empirical facts about elements? Or is it to be treated as the product of a theory of the structure of atoms, which predicts patterns of facts about elements? Is it to be shown historically as built up piece by piece though nevertheless under a large guiding vision, or is it to be provided as something 'given', a familiar classificatory tool of chemists to be used before being understood? Thus in this case, the nature of the subject matter does not determine the form of explanation, but poses difficult problems for it to solve.

Chapter 7

'STYLES' OF EXPLAINING

Integrating performances

In Chapters 2 to 5 we set out and exemplified the components of our framework for describing explanations, our 'language of description'. So we focused on the necessary components of explanation: the production of 'difference', the construction of entities, the transformation of knowledge and the imposing of meaning on matter, each in separate chapters. In Chapter 6 we looked at a number of important contextual influences on how explanations turn out. But of course explanations rest on the *simultaneous* deployment, implementation, performance of all of these, all at the one time. In this chapter we will show how all these things come together in a complete performance. To do this, we use somewhat longer pieces of our transcripts, so as to look at these complete performances. The focus will now be on how things are put together, where the emphasis lies, what strategies are used, and what skills have to be deployed to sustain them.

We will identify a number of 'styles' of explanation. A 'style' of explanation is not to be thought of as a personal property of a teacher, though one could become habitual. It is more a way of consistently approaching the job of explanation, from a particular angle. Some significant examples of such 'styles', taken from our observations, include:

- *'Let's think it through together'*: explanations are arrived at through the teacher's collecting and reshaping ideas from the class.
- *'The teller of tales'*: an explanation is offered as like a story, with plot and subplots, using some of the devices of narrative.

- *'Say it my way'*: explanatory forms of words are laid out by the teacher and practised by the class.
- *'See it my way'*: starting from a given scientific theory, facts and phenomena are rationalized in terms of that theory.

Thus in this chapter we present a rough taxonomy of some ways in which explaining can be done, and discuss the consequences of each, for what might be achieved and for how it positions pupils with respect to knowledge.

'Let's think it through together'

One way to achieve explanations is by the teacher collecting and shaping ideas offered by students. Clearly, students' contributions are crucial: they are the actual material out of which explanations are going to be carved. They also, of course, provide the ongoing interaction which the teacher has to handle – something we discussed in Chapter 6. Thus this way of working towards an explanation places great demands on the teacher's skill. The teacher has to start students off, to stimulate further contributions, to feed in additional ideas, and to make clear what status is being given to students' ideas – are they being welcomed, being clarified or modified, or are they now being made part of the final account? This involves continuous movements between, for example, opening up opportunities for contributions, and framing and 'making official' material which has been offered.

Our example, previewed in Chapter 1, is a Year 10 lesson about skeletal joints. The fact that joints are places where bones move against each other has already been established in previous lessons. The lesson as a whole starts with a test, proceeds to discuss the design of a good joint, and then considers how to categorize different types of joint. We will focus here on the second stage, in which the teacher – Leon – gets the class to put together a picture of what ought to go into an ideal joint. His initial questions suggest both the problem – the wearing away of bones – and establish the exploratory tone of what is to come. By starting from a rather wide definition of a joint (two bone surfaces which move against each other), and asking in general what can go wrong with them, he opens up a wide range of possibilities for thinking.

Leon: Okay [ ] Let's just talk about it in– first of all the principle of the joints. What is the problem if you've got two bones that you want to move against each other – what's goin–, what's the – what's going to be the big problem at the end where the? – imagine how many times

Student: They'll wear away.

Leon: you must move your elbow, yeah? So write it down. Okay? [*Starts dictation pace and intonation*] Where [ ] two [ ] bone [ ] surfaces [ ] where two bone surfaces [ ] move [ ] against [ ] each other [ ] the danger is [ ] they will wear away [*stops dictating*] . . . it's obvious, yeah . . . They have to be hard don't they, or they'll wear away? How – how do we – Charlene how can we get round it, surely, how can we get round it, they're gonna wear away, they've got to be hard in order, 'cause, you know, like, we're big and heavy, yeah, gotta be hard, but if they're hard they're gonna rub up- rub away, aren't they? Yeah. Charlene what do you think? Stop the wearing away, something, what can you do, to de– to reduce it?

The lesson proceeds with the teacher skilfully rephrasing, refocusing, and teasing out ideas presented by the students. This is often done by means of questioning around what a joint can do or have done to it (the potentials of this entity). Consequences of students' ideas are followed up. Analogies they suggest, which help them envisage what is involved in the anatomy of a joint by comparing it to more familiar mechanisms, are picked up and elaborated. But, once ideas have been collected and brought to a possible conclusion, Leon changes gear. He gives the idea that they reach (namely that joints must be lubricated) new status by deciding to dictate it back to the class for insertion in their notebooks. What was a moment ago a 'possible good idea' of some students has been turned into communal 'textbook knowledge'. It is now 'knowledge for remembering', and vocabulary for future use.

Leon: Let's try and stop the wearing away. How can we stop the wearing away? Emma, how can we stop the wearing away?
Emma: [*Inaudible*]
Leon: Yes?
Emma: Put a sheet of something between it.
Leon: Yeah what sort of sheet?
Student: Tissues.
Student: No, no, that'd be like,
Leon: That's rough isn't it.
Student: [*Inaudible*]
Student: I know.
Student: Perhaps an elastic band.
Student: No, a flat sheet, between 'em, a disc or something.
Leon: And what would the disc do, instead of rubbing on– ?
Student: It'd stop them hitting each other.
Leon: So instead of rubbing on each other they're rubbing on this, like, plastic thing?
Student: Yeah, but they . . .
Student: Fluids, like fluids, yeah.
Leon: Some sort of, what would fluids do though?
Student: [*All talking together*]
Student: They stop 'em rubbing it.
Leon: Like oil.
Student: But your weight'd be moving, your weight'd be doing that [*gestures*].

Leon: Like oil?

Student: Like oil, like they show it in the car advert.

Leon: In a car, what, what does the, what does the oil do in the car, what's it for?

Student: Lubricate the car.

Leon: So in the car, think about it, your hard things are rubbing against each other, but if you put oil in, a tiny thin layer, a bit like molecule-like ball bearings, yeah, in-between the two, so instead of rubbing against each other, what, they're just rolling on these molecule size ball bearings yes. So do they get really hot and wear away? No, because they're just rolling instead of scraping. So what could you have in a joint?

Student: Oil.

Leon: Some sort of oil stuff. So let's write it down, right. So this is like things we could do. Have some, write it down [*starts speaking with dictation speed and intonation*] we could have something like oil [ ] we could have something like oil to lubricate yeah [ ] we could have something like oil to lubricate [ ]

Student: How do you spell that?

Leon: L U B R I C A T E [*dictates again*] to lubricate the joints [ ] we could have something like oil [ ] to lubricate the joint [*stops dictating*] [ ] Okay, that'll do, so that would make the movement a little smoother wouldn't it?

Further problems, arising naturally as an outcome of the proposed solution for the original problem at hand, are often suggested by the teacher, though students are encouraged to have a go. But these suggestions are always made to appear to arise naturally from the discussion; as consequences of what has just been proposed. In this way the discussion, while skilfully led by the teacher, has a feeling of continuity and of dialogue. Here is Leon introducing a difficulty with the idea of 'oily stuff':

Leon: Excuse me, how do you stop all that oil stuff just spilling out?

Student: Put something round it.

Students: [*Several speak at once*]

Leon: So like another layer around the whole thing to keep the oily stuff in. Like seal it or something.

Student: Yes, seal it.

Leon: OK right then, then we could have – er – and it has to be like a bit flexible [ ] a flexible seal – **should I say seal or cover or what?**

Student: Cover.

Leon: [*Slowly with emphasis*] Flexible cover around the whole joint [ ] to keep the oily fluid in – to keep the oily fluid in. [ ] We're well on the way to making a reasonable joint at the moment.

Leon has to decide what to follow up and what to skip, without, however, dismissing contributions in a way which will inhibit students from making others. Notice Leon asking the class what to dictate back to them ('should I say . . . ?'). Many of the students' contributions are offered as metaphors (oil, seal). Indeed the task of 'thinking it through together' is done through much metaphorical work. It involves trying out ideas, imagining consequences, asking 'what if?' questions, and generally playing mentally with various known entities and mechanisms to see if they might fit. For example, Leon points out that the 'oily stuff' might seep out. Comparing the joint with a car, a student suggests a tube to feed in more oil. Leon offers an equally common-sense objection:

> *Student*: We need some how of getting in there – we need a tube.
> *Leon*:   You need to somehow get in there either a tube coming in – but if you had a tube coming in – think about it – when you bend the joint what might happen to the tube? It might break or nick or–

This continues until all the essential features of a joint have been identified. So pleased is Leon with the way his strategy has worked, that he allows himself a punning joke to underline what has been achieved.

> *Leon*: So we've actually – I mean I don't know how we did it – but we've actually built a perfect joint. We've actually done a perfect joint. So when your mum says 'Who's doing Sunday dinner?' you can say 'me', because in class on Wednesday I did a perfect joint.

'The teller of tales'

The 'teller of tales' uses the seductive form of narrative to carry students along. Our example is a lesson about digestion and the digestive system, with a mixed-ability Year 10 class. The teacher (David) has several things to achieve. As we noted in Chapter 3, digestion is at one level an entirely familiar everyday process. But as a biological process, it involves looking at what goes on in the body, and so at the parts of the body themselves, in quite novel ways. Furthermore, all the new ideas – the functions and structures of organs, what happens to food – are interlocking. Each needs the others in order to make sense. The strategy David chooses is to use stories to carry essential structures of knowledge.

> *David*: Now let me tell you, as we're going through these bits, I'm going to tell you little stories, about the various bits that we're talking about.

Amongst the things David has to do is to get students to rethink what food is, and what happens to it as it enters and leaves the body. Familiar steak and butter will become the generic substances protein and fat, and these in turn will be re-imagined as complicated molecular structures. The inside of the body becomes a structure of tubes, walls and fluids; a drastic transformation we saw David effecting for the earthworm in Chapter 1.

David: This gut, the hole that goes through – the gut, is a hole going through the middle of the animal, and in the same way the tube that goes through you – starts at the mouth and ends with the anus – is just a hole going through the middle. Now you're putting food into this hole, right, and the earthworm is putting food into this hole. Somehow the food has got to get out of the hole and into the worm.

. . .

Now, these bits here, the – the leaves and – and all the other bits that the earthworm's eating, and all the bits you're eating, are made up of proteins and fats and carbohydrates and so on. The problem is that the molecules, the molecules that make up the food are co–, are long and complicated. For example, we said that . . . if you look at a starch molecule for example, which is what you get in potatoes, and what you get in – in pasta, and what you get in starch food, is made up of more than twenty-four bits, joined together like this, and the walls of this tube, okay, is like a piece of netting – is like a piece of netting, okay, these long tubes – sorry, these long molecules – are so big that they won't fit through the net to get to blood on the other side . . . The food has to get out of the tube, through the wall of the gut, into the blood circuit and be taken around the body, okay. But these molecules are so big that they won't fit through. So what the body has to do is to break them down into small bits – break them down into small bits . . . so that we finish up with small simple little molecules and the small simple little molecules can go though the tube, through the wall of the gut into the blood and be then taken off to your cells and your muscles so the food can actually be used, yes?

What David has done is to strip digestion down to the barest essentials: a tube through which food goes and in which it must be broken down. This provides a theoretical backbone, so to speak, which will – as he tells the stories which follow – hold the argument together. Further, the narrative form can, as we pointed out in Chapter 4, 'carry' knowledge in the very structure of the story and in its use of analogy and metaphor (as in 'netting' above).

In his first story, David, having established the crucial role of the stomach in digesting protein, is about to make sure this specific function is not forgotten. He does so through a surprising suggestion:

David: Most of the food that gets digested in your stomach is protein, so the meat and fish and that kind of stuff gets digested in your stomach. But would you believe that you can actually survive without your stomach?

The story which he is about to tell does several jobs at the same time. It functions as evidence. It is highly memorable, providing a ready reminder of the fact 'the stomach digests protein'. And it connects this fact to other matters of concern, such as radiation damage and cancer. A small fact about digestion is linked to a much wider view of life and of biology. For these reasons, he gives his story – which is really only a subplot of the narrative of the whole lesson, plenty of space.

David: Do you all know the film star called John Wayne?

Students: Yeah.

David: Yeah? John Wayne. This is a long story, settle down, it's a long story. John Wayne, was making a film in the nineteen forties, and when he was making the film in the nineteen forties, they were testing the atomic bombs in the valley next to the one, they were making a western film, so it would be a film in, you know, the Wild West, and – and, John Wayne was kind of filming with, with all the cameramen and all the other stars, and so on and so forth, in a valley here, and about five miles away they were, they were testing atomic bombs, and it just happened that day the wind was blowing in this direction, and they didn't know at the time but a whole load of atomic radiation, it came off the bombs and was blown across, arr, to where these people were working, and they didn't know, you don't see atomic radiation, you don't suddenly go, 'Oh look, a big cloud of atomic radiation,' it just happens, but you know, every single person who worked on that film set died of cancer, within the next twenty or thirty years, right. So atomic radiation, as you probably all know, is something which eventually causes cancers, and every single person who was working on that film set that day, eventually died of cancer, and the cancer which John Wayne got was cancer of the stomach.

Explaining through storytelling often involves keeping track of complicated plots, with many asides and changes in level. The pace may vary. It may be speeded up or slowed down depending on how often students join in, either with questions or with contributions. Or the teacher may decide to make space for explaining something else. The story is going to be about the surgical removal of Wayne's stomach. But David here opts to break off to provide extra information.

David: Now, if you've got cancer of the stomach, umm, in this case, what can you do? Well, you can cure cancers in three ways. Well, you can cure cancers in three ways, the best way – Oh, well, first of all, let's see what cancer is

Student: Cysts.

David: is where a cell, just one cell, for some reason, sort of goes mad, and instead of just dividing, to make new cells – you know, if you cut yourself, then the cell dies, but other cells divide to make new cells – that's what should happen, if I damage the skin I get new skin cells, if I damage a muscle I get new muscle cells, if I damage a stomach I get new stomach cells. But in a cancer, one cell divides, it just goes mad, it doesn't make the right cells, it just makes more, and more, and more cells, and you get a lump, or a cyst. Now one way to live, to – to – to deal with a cancer – if it's small enough, early enough, is to cut it out and throw it away. Later on, you can try and attack the bad cells, with, with chemicals, called drugs, or [ ] with atomic radiation [ ] but stomach cancers, because the stomach's got no nerves in it, you don't really notice you've got stomach cancer until sometimes it's too late, to do anything about it.

It is clear that explaining through story-telling follows no simple linear form. Here, within the 'story of digestion', another story is embedded (John Wayne), within which there are further stories (a radiation accident). Also, different modes of explaining may co-exist. So far, in our example, part of the explaining can be done in a straightforward factual way (cancers are the result of uncontrolled replication) and partly through the telling of stories.

The resolution of the story again relies on the conceptual 'backbone' (digestive system as a tube) and recruits everyday knowledge ('connect it up to the rest of the tubing'):

David: What they did with John Wayne, was to cut his whole stomach out. And he lived for another ten years after that, he died when he was kind of eighty or something like that, he, you know, he was an old man when he died, but he'd had his stomach, his whole stomach removed, and they took just that bit of the tubing there

Student: But –

David: connected it up to the rest of the tubing, and [ ] the job of the stomach is to digest, mainly is to digest protein, and the rest of the system could manage without the stomach. John was vegetarian when, you know, really a vegetarian, yeah, so, so basically, he survived.

The overall message carried by the story (stomachs digest proteins) is preserved despite the detours into other matters. Stories have a robust structure and yet are flexible enough to accommodate additions or omissions.

Later in the same lesson, David tells another story. It is the story of the fur-trapper who accidentally shot a hole in his stomach, a part of which we used in Chapter 2 when thinking about creating difference. Here we reproduce it in full, because we are interested, precisely, in showing the whole 'performance'. So, it is the story of an accident, followed by a surprisingly unexpected course of events which led to an increase in scientific knowledge. As a teaching device, it is not only an example of producing difference through surprise, but also one of 'insinuating knowledge' on the back of a truly gripping if macabre story. Contained in it are messages about the origin and nature of scientific knowledge, as well as knowledge about how the stomach functions.

David: I've told you the story about the trapper haven't I?

Student 1: Mmm.

Student 2: No.

David: Ohhh, haven't I told you about Alexis St. Martin yet?

Students: No.

David: Oh, that's a good one. Right, okay, listen to this, this is how
people, this is how people learnt what happens inside the
stomach, right. I told you last week, about the Italian man,
didn't I?, who was feeding himself bits of sponge, so, and he
was collecting the sponge and wringing it out, and he found
that by taking the, the contents of the stomach, wringing it
out over meat . . . you know, this research was going on maybe
two hundred years ago when people were first of all discovering what was going on in these, arr, these things [*pats his
own stomach*], and one of these blokes who discovered ever
such a lot about what was happening inside the stomach,
was a doctor called Doctor Beaumont, who worked in a fort
in Canada, right. You see what happened was, there was a
trapper – Canada is a really really big place, Canada used to
– used to make, two hundred years ago – Canada used to make
all its money by trapping animals, skinning them, and selling
the furs, right. They had a massive fur trade, in Canada two
hundred years ago, and one of the trappers was a Frenchman
called Alexis St. Martin. Now Alexis St. Martin must have been
a bit of a useless trapper, because one day he went out with
his gun, and instead of shooting a beaver he shot himself,

Students: [*Laughter*]

David: and he managed to shoot himself right here, through the
stomach, blew a great big hole, through his stomach, and
the bullet went out the back, took a bit of his back away as
well, and left a – a big hole all the way through here. Anyway,
he wrapped himself up, and he was conscious, he wrapped
himself up, and he went back to the fort.

The unexpected sequence of events catches attention and makes the story
memorable. However, by providing counterintuitive developments, the teacher
is not merely producing an element of surprise. He is confronting students
with their current knowledge and understanding about the human body and
creating the necessary difference to integrate new information which will
result in new meanings to be constructed. The difference produced here is
so vast however, in so many ways, that first of all the students focus on that
factor: is this yarn even credible?

Student: **Is this true?**

David: This is a true story yes, he went back to the fort, and he went,
uh, to the, to the doctor in the fort, and said, 'Look doctor, I
have shot a big hole through myself,' and the doctor said, 'Oh
get awa–, oh yes, you have, haven't you, ho-ho,' and then he

said, err, he must have said to his assistant, 'This bloke ain't gonna survive, look how much, he's blown half his gut away here.' So he – he put him to bed, and he wrapped him up, and he left him to die, and the next morning he came back and Alexis St. Martin was still alive. So he must have changed the bandages and looked through this big hole, and thought, 'Oh blimey,' you know, 'What next?.' Anyway, he left this bloke without trying to stitch him up, 'cause he thought, well, the bloke was going to die. Then he realised the bloke was actually going to live, so, after a couple of days, the doctor started to try and stitch him up, but he'd left it so long, that the hole, where the bloke'd blown through the skin, and through the stomach here, the hole, had – had, started to heal, it hadn't healed properly, and, and the skin had stuck to the hole in the – in the stomach, so he tried to stitch it up, but as much as he tried he couldn't, he left a hole there. So he – he bandaged it up, and after about a week or so the bloke was still alive, and he had this big hole that poked through into his stomach, so the doctor, must have said to him, 'I'm sorry about this, you know, I didn't expect you to live, a bit unfortunate, you've got this big hole there, haven't y–, but you'll be alright won't you, you can just walk around with a big bandage stuck on here, and just, you know, don't lean forward when you eat your breakfast, 'cause it'll all fall out, you'll be alright.' And then suddenly the doctor thought, 'Wait a minute, this means I could look through that hole, and see what's happening to the food while it's being digested.'

Student: Oh, and he could see.

What follows next is an explanation of a systematic, controlled (though unorthodox) 'scientific' procedure, given through an account which is clearly meant to fit in with similar descriptions or personal experiences of students when carrying out tests in science.

David: That's right, so he said to this bloke, he said, 'Look, why don't – why don't you just stay here for a few days, and – you know – just have free breakfasts now and again, and I'll just have a look thr– look through this hole, and see what happened to your breakfast as you're eating it?' So they did this, and the doctor wrote these great long diaries of what was happening, he took bits of – he took bits of boiled egg, for example, and tied the bit of boiled egg onto a bit of string, stuck it through the hole, and then he st– took the time, 'Eight o'clock', 'ni-', you know, 'nine o'clock', stuck a boiled egg through, [*mimes waiting*] 'five past nine', pulled it out, had a look, to see what was happening, wrote down what was happening, stuck it back in. And he did this for day after day after day, with all sorts of different foods, sticking it through the hole, pulling it out, looking to see what was going on. And this was – eventually what happened was that Alexis St. Martin got fed up with it and he ran away, and er, Doctor Beaumont was so worried about having lost his err, having lost his subject, that he chased after him, and went down, you know, in one of the main cities, and said, 'Oh no, look, come on, I'll pay you more money to come and do some more experiments,' so they did this for, I don't know, about six months or so. The bloke lived, presumably, after that, with his bandage to stop his breakfast dropping out.

The humorous touch at the end helps with the transition from the story telling mode and signals the summary of what has been said, bringing the focus back to the biological topic in hand and away from the peculiarities of the story, and returning to a direct information-giving mode.

David: Anyway, that's how they discovered what was happening inside the stomach. When you've got – so what've I said – so far, I've said food gets chewed up, goes down through the gullet, into the stomach, stays in the stomach for about eight hours, by the time it's been in the stomach for about eight hours it's turned to liquid, and then the stomach squeezes, and squirts, the liquid food on, and it goes into the first little bit of the small intestine, which is called the duodenum.

Displayed in this form, this story may seem an uneconomical way of teaching, though we believe not. A very large number of relevant elements and structures have been introduced, and in a truly riveting fashion. This story is sufficient bandage to stop this set of knowledge from dropping out. The teacher's last remarks call attention back to the main story about the digestive system, its components and the process of digestion.

The story in its entirety illustrates a general point we have made before, about explanation existing at different scales. Here we have another example of nested and of juxtaposed structures of explanation. The lesson starts with framing the problem in simplified terms (what happens to food as it goes through this hole). The stories then explain what part of the digestive system does and how we know about it. Within and alongside them we find extra explanations, for example about cancers. The whole explanation structure creates a lesson in which the understanding of entities and processes of the digestive system emerges in an integrated way. The whole thing replaces what might have been a list of parts and functions of the digestive system with a dynamic account of just these parts and functions worked into narratives.

It is also clear from the above account that narratives like this, perhaps surprisingly, have essentially the functions of *demonstration*, as we discussed them in Chapter 5. They make material events serve a theoretical picture; they invest material fact with meaning.

'Say it my way'

Another style of explaining is to focus on 'the right way to talk about things'. We have chosen an example concerning the right way to talk about sound waves – an example already discussed in Chapter 4, as an instance of 'didactic transposition'. It comes from a Year 8 class in an all-girls school.

The teacher (Alan) has shown the students different sounds associated with different images on the screen of a cathode-ray oscilloscope. Now, at this stage something new happens: the transformation of sound into a new entity. A space for new meanings is opened up, when sound is transformed into something to be seen, not heard. Alan's efforts concentrate on making the students talk about what they hear in terms of what they see.

> *Alan*:   Now then, the cathode-ray oscilloscope can't display them like that, so how does it try to display the different types of sound. Yes?
>
> *Student*: . . . by making different lines and different shapes.
>
> *Alan*:   Okay different lines different shapes. You should see if we get a nice pure note you should see a nice s– smooth wave like that [*gesture of sinusoidal wave*] going across the screen.

A further level of complexity is to be added, however. Changes in what is heard become changes in what is seen, but these are also to be described in a new language. The next stage involves paying attention to selected aspects of the images seen on the screen and describing what you see in a particular way. Changes like those in the pitch of the sound and in the corresponding shape of the trace on the screen, are given linguistic forms which link them.

> *Alan*:   Now then, if the sound gets louder, what happens to the trace that we see on the screen? Yes?
>
> *Student*: It gets higher.
>
> *Alan*:   Okay. The trace gets higher. Okay? Now then, technically speaking using the correct words, what happens to the amplitude of the sound? Yes?
>
> *Student*: It increases.
>
> *Alan*:   It increases. Brilliant.
>
> . . .
>
> *Alan*:   If the sound became quieter what would happen to the amplitude? Yes?
>
> *Student*: It would decrease.
>
> *Alan*:   It would decrease. Good.

The language is one in which what is seen is not sound, but 'the trace', but in which the sound makes the trace. So the trace is described in simple observational terms ('It gets higher'). Then this is translated into another more theoretical language, to do with 'amplitude'. The trace getting higher is not merely a trace getting higher; it has *meaning* – that an amplitude has increased. Next a linguistic form to link sound directly to amplitude is worked on. The language being developed here derives from a culture which routinely says things like, 'Large amplitude sounds . . .'. Such links, including that between loudness and amplitude, are practised and rehearsed several times at this point in the lesson. But after a time, Alan simply starts using them interchangeably. Instead of the language saying directly that the two are connected, it shifts to treating them as alternatives. Thus Alan, without making any remark about it, rephrases a sentence about one in terms of the other:

Alan: Is the amplitude changing there? [ ]
Student: No.
Alan: No, the loudness is not changing. All that is changing is the frequency – all that is changing is the frequency OK?

On the surface, it may seem that very little has changed for the students' understanding. However, by using either term in the same sequence of exchanges, Alan is modifying in a quite dramatic way the meaning of the 'height of the trace' which his students see on the screen. A visual–abstract meaning has been constructed for an everyday auditory experience.

Rephrasing

Rephrasing and rewording play a crucial part in the explanation of the new terms being introduced as part of the new way of talking about sound. Alan puts a lot of work into building up meanings for terms by using them – and getting students to use them – in various ways. He continually shifts the linguistic ground; having said something one way, another is tried, sometimes in the direction of greater elaboration or complexity (from 'distance between a peak and a peak' to 'distance . . . between any two corresponding points'). Sometimes Alan just changes how something is said ('they get wider', 'they get spread out'), but sometimes he explicitly signals a change ('let me put it in a different way'). Here the explicit signal heralds a definition-statement.

Alan: As the sound goes [speaking in a low pitch voice] lower, what happens?
Student: They get wider.
Alan: They get spread out. Now then, what measurement can we make on those waves? What can we actually – let me put it in a different way. You drew out a wave. OK? You said that the distance between a peak and a peak or between a trough and a trough had a certain name. Can anyone remember what that name is? Yes.
Student: [Inaudible] wavelength.
Alan: The wavelength – the distance between two peaks or two troughs or any two corresponding points on the wavy lines. If the sound is going to get higher we've already said that the waves are going to get squashed, closer together, so what is actually happening to the wave length? Is it increasing or decreasing?

Student 1: They're increasing.
Student 2: [*Inaudible*] decreasing.
Alan: The distance between two peaks?
Student 1: Decreasing.
Alan: OK. Good. I thought you knew the answer to that. So the wavelength is decreasing as the frequency or pitch is increasing.

Typically of the style 'Say it my way', after a period of such successive rephrasings, Alan moves to crystallize them into an 'official' version which is dictated to the whole class or written on the blackboard to be recorded in the students' books.

Alan: We basically were wanting to finish with a few sentences that will say [*starts speaking with a slow impressive tone*] when a sound becomes louder, the amplitude increases; when the sound become quieter, the amplitude decreases; the sound becomes higher, the wavelength decreases; the sound becomes lower, the wavelength increases. [*Speech returns to normal*] OK. Has anybody got all of those down?

Is this just a word-game?

In 'Say it my way' the task necessarily involves explaining new terms. But it cannot be merely a word-game using new words to label new ideas; no such game could work. Work has to be done grounding new terms, often in action or in metaphor. In the present case, the new terms can be grounded in the visual representation of sounds on the screen, and their associated metaphors (see Chapter 4). Work has also always to be done relating new terms one to another. Indeed this is the essential part of the work to be done, because a specific 'way of talking' is such just by virtue of making ideas hang together in certain specific ways. The sentence, 'The amplitude has a high pitch' makes no sense because its ideas are disconnected. Its English grammar is fine; its 'scientific grammar' is hopeless. Learning the 'scientific grammar' is learning to 'Say it my way'.

In this final extract we seem to see Alan going through a rather mechanical exercise in sentence construction (text in SMALL CAPITALS corresponds to the word written on the board as well as spoken):

Alan: [*Speaking aloud, making long pauses, as he writes on the whiteboard*] AS A SOUND [ ] BECOMES LOUDER, [ ] THE AMPLITUDE [ ] remind me what the amplitude does? [ ]
Student: Gets higher.
Alan: Higher or how could we? – what word would fit into that sentence? [ ]
Student: Increases.
Alan: It increases, good. So the amplitude [ ] INCREASES, good. Number 2 [ ] AS A SOUND BECOMES [ ] QUIETER [ ] sh shhhh [ ] THE AMPLITUDE [ ] What does the amplitude do? The word that will fit into that sentence. DECREASES.

These sentences do an important job. They relate percepts ('sound becomes louder') to concepts ('amplitude increases'). Correspondingly, adjectives describing perceptions ('louder') become verbs describing what an abstract entity is doing ('amplitude' is 'increasing'). The question, 'What word would fit into that sentence?' asks not merely for a suitable word, but for a new word of a new kind – for a new way of seeing as well as a new way of saying.

This new knowledge has much latent power, of which Alan – if not yet the students – will be well aware. The terms 'amplitude', 'frequency', 'wavelength', etc. are destined to be transformed into variables whose values describe waves, and whose relationships will be represented in yet further formal systems, starting with equations and graphs. 'The sounds one hears' are part-way though a massive transformation, from a world of immediate perception to one of abstract formalization. It is this, rather than just getting students to 'say it right', which in the end motivates this kind of lesson.

But there is a price to pay. Alan's students are not, and cannot be, party to this vision of where 'saying it his way' is headed. He cannot easily tell them, because it is very difficult to envisage having a new way of talking, and so of thinking, before one has it. The advantages cannot be seen before they are experienced. So there is a real danger that students subjected to the style 'Say it my way' will see it as no more than exactly that.

'See it my way'

Some kinds of explaining need somehow to enforce a special vision of the world. It is this which we have called 'See it my way'. To illustrate it, we focus on another lesson by David – which helps to make the point that what we are describing here are ways of doing explaining and not particular personal styles. This lesson (in Year 10) is about plate tectonics. David starts with a promise:

> *David*: . . . I've said to you that there's something which is really quite simple . . . I want you to try and understand this today, as I said, I think it's dead simple, and it's kind of, like, you know, the government has committed an error to put this on, on level ten, because it's too simple for level ten, on the other hand, if you understand this . . . if there are questions in the exam, then you're in business because it's so straightforward.

Here David uses one of the simpler and cruder forms of creating difference which we considered in Chapter 2: utility in relation to schooling. Actually, what he has to explain is not easy at all. It depends on reaching a whole new and unsettling view of the Earth, not as a stable permanent home but as active and moving under one's feet. So he has to get his students to see things in a different way. He begins with a curious fact whose explanation seems to call for the continents to move:

David: And I think people began to realise, during the course of this century, that when they looked at the map of the Earth, it looked pretty obviously, as if, kind of, bits fitted together.

David shows them a map – a rather unusual one in which mountains and valleys under the sea are as prominent as those on land. It is not even too easy to see the familiar forms of continents, and David spends time pointing them out. Why is he doing this? In the style 'See it my way' there is generally an explanation waiting to be given, which is what decides what phenomena are counted as interesting. And David has such an explanation – the moving of continental plates over the Earth's surface. Thus in the next extract he concentrates on one phenomenon for which that explanation will be able to account.

David: So the map is quite complex . . . First let's look at the spots of land in the middles of all this mess. Here's America in the middle [*teacher shapes out the Americas with his finger*]. [ ] Over here is Britain, a bit of Europe here, a bit of Africa down there. Now, all the different colours [ ] on the Earth's surface, are what kind of rocks are being formed where. [ ] But what I just wanted to show you, huh, it's very difficult to show you, is this bit down here, where this bit sticks out here [*the teacher shapes out a bit of South America*], can you see this bit of South America sticks, sticks out here, and just here, look, there's this sort of bit of Africa that's got this kind of armpit, and if you look at these two, you can think to yourself, well look, that bit fits in there, that's convenient, isn't it, how come there's just, you know, a thousand miles of ocean in the middle, but that bit looks like it fits in there?

Here then we illustrate again a point made first in Chapter 1, that what gets explained depends on what explanations are ready and waiting. If in science itself, phenomena can be envisaged as in need of explanation, in teaching science it is almost the other way round. The existence of explanations decides what questions get asked. The existence of an answer is the reason for posing the question. David makes the question more real by describing how the ideas evolved, starting with the now discredited idea that mountains formed by the folding of the crust of a cooling and shrinking Earth.

David: Now, through the course of the nineteen twenties people thought what was going on, was, as the planet is cooling down, it was forming a skin on the surface, and as it cooled down more, and it cooled down more, and it cooled down more, it started to shrink [*holds his hands in a ball and 'shrinks' it*] and as it started to shrink, the skin on the surface, started to form itself up into, into, into folds, and bends, and contours, and that's the way, they believed, in which the mountains were formed. They were cooling down and then crinkling up and forming this, this cold crinkled lump, OK? Basically, through the nineteen twenties people began to

> realise this really wasn't very satisfactory because it did not really
> explain how come you have continents and how come you have
> oceans and so on and so forth.

David has tried to get them to see the Earth in one way. The language is
very vivid, concrete and active. And it needs to be: it is not easy to see the
Alps as wrinkled skin on custard. In 'See it my way', facts are rationalized
in terms of a theory. And this theory, as we suggested above, may change
the world to be explained, pointing to new phenomena and new questions
about them. David now needs to get them to see the Earth in yet another
new way, in which enormous plates move and drift. He cannot appeal to
observed fact, to demonstration, or to logical argument. He must appeal to
imagination, and use every resource he can to make it real. What he does
is to use a lot of gesture, using his hands to mimic the possible movements
of continents.

> *David*: And gradually over the course of the sort of last ten to twenty
> years people have begun to realize what is going on. And what is
> going on is pretty simple, but on the other hand, is very massive.
> It's so massive that it is quite difficult to understand it, because
> we are talking about great chunks of the Earth moving around.
> What is going on is this. As the planet cooled down these lumps
> of – of the skin of rock that's formed on the surface of the planet
> has – has cooled, yes?, but they haven't formed one single lump.
> They formed a series of individual plates. So there's a cool plate
> of rock here [*holds out one hand*] and a plate here [*holds out the
> other hand*] and those plates of rock are moving [*moves the hands*]
> . . . They'll move in three different possible ways. One is the plates
> which are sitting together [*puts two hands edge to edge*] and, every
> now and again, they shift like this [*slides one hand along beside the
> other*]. These are called 'conservative margins' [*said slowly and
> solemnly – a technical term*]. Although if you lived on one of these
> plates you wouldn't think it was too conservative at all. A pair of
> plates against – like that [*puts hands edge to edge again*] and just
> occasionally shifting, are things which cause earthquakes all over
> the world. So little movements of these plates, when the plates
> just move against each, other cause earthquakes [*moves hands again*]
> . . . in 1906 the whole of San Francisco was destroyed by one of
> these 'little conservative movements' [*said ironically*].

Later the gestures are even more vivid. David symbolizes what happens
when one plate dives under another by sliding one hand below the other
and then pushing fingers of the lower hand up through fingers of the upper
hand to represent molten rock rising and making volcanoes. That David's
appeal is basically to the imagination is shown by the fact that he has a
demonstration to show to illustrate convection in the interior of the Earth,
but that he doesn't much care if it works – and it doesn't. We described his
'failed' demonstration in Chapter 5.

This is, perhaps, a rather special case of the style 'See it my way'. At least what has to be seen in a special new way – the Earth – is and remains a concrete object. Seeing in a new way becomes even more important in other areas of science in which entities have their basic nature altered. Obvious examples include matter being made mostly of empty space, or diseases being caused not by circumstances but by germs. When it comes – in much later learning – to gravity being just curved space, the need to see things in someone else's way becomes the heart and whole of the problem.

Chapter 8

WHAT NOW, AND
WHAT NEXT?

Concluding and looking forward

In this final chapter, we will try to draw the threads of the book together, describing what we think we have done, summarizing our underlying assumptions, explaining what claims we wish to make, and looking forward to what might need to come next.

A fundamental problem to be faced in trying to describe explanations in the science classroom (or for that matter any kind of communication) is that many things are necessarily going on at once. That is just how communication *works*. Quite generally, whenever one communicates, there is (at least) something to say, some position to be taken with respect to others, and some structuring and organizing of the communication to be done. These and other things happen all at the same time, in a kind of polyphony. The consequence is that any explanation has to be described on several dimensions at once. This is how we see the component parts of our account of explanations working.

When, therefore, we identify the four main tasks, of opening up difference, constructing entities, transforming knowledge, and making matter meaningful, we do *not* suppose that these happen 'one after the other'. On the contrary, they all happen together all the time, as we suggested in Chapter 7. So teachers do not in some simple sequence first establish a need for an explanation, then construct the entities to do the job, using scientific knowledge transformed for the purpose, finally reaching an account which gives a new meaning to material events. But they do do all of these things, and the contribution of each needs to be described. If some of the time what teachers do looks more like one of these dimensions than like the others, the others are always there in the background.

It was for this reason that, when introducing these ideas in Chapter 1, we could draw so heavily on a very few examples. If that seemed forced at a first reading, it may be useful to reconsider the issue now. We could, for example, treat the case of explaining the gut of an earthworm as opening up a different way of seeing things, as work towards constructing the entity 'digestive system', and as transforming a biological structure into a piece of topology, using devices such as analogy. All were there to be seen, in a few minutes of speech and a diagram, and all working together as opposed to being strung in a chain.

In broad terms, then, what we believe we have done is to identify – from a particular semiotic point of view – some main aspects of what must be involved in any act of explaining science in the classroom, and then to illustrate in considerable detail how these very general aspects can be seen and described in particular cases and how they can then be used to compare and contrast cases. Further, in Chapters 6 and 7, we have sought to show how in different contexts, with different people, explaining different things, the dynamics of the situation issue in a variety of ways of doing the job of explaining – different strategies or styles. Despite their differences, however, each style still has an account at the same general level – the level of what any kind of explaining has to do.

Assumptions

In all this work, we have started from a number of broad assumptions about the nature of communication and of scientific explanations. These were outlined in Chapter 1, but it may be helpful to summarize them again here.

We take communication to be continuously active, transformative or constructive. We do not accept a view of communication as using fixed terms to refer to fixed realities. For us, each meaning made is in some measure a new meaning, not an old one reshuffled in a repetitive game of saying the same things over again. Those with something to say are necessarily always saying something new, sometimes radically, often only slightly. Those with something to understand have necessarily to make that understanding anew for themselves, again only sometimes radically but always to some extent. It is from this that communication gets its dynamism and the source of its continuous transformation and change.

We also take communication to be integrated and multimodal. In the past and still in many respects today, our Western culture takes language to be the dominant mode of communication, and within that gives pride of place to writing over speaking. Other modes of communication, especially graphic and pictorial modes, are generally thought of as adjuncts to the 'real thing' – as members of a supporting cast. Much evidence, from the dominance of television to the widespread use of images in advertising and in signs, points in the opposite direction. At least, we believe, full attention has to be paid to them on a par with language. And we include in these other modes of communication gesture and actions. Our assumption is that communication involves several such modes, integrated together, each performing a special and significant role.

We also start from a set of assumptions about the nature of scientific explanation; a position set out in Chapter 1 and used repeatedly throughout the book. Until recently, the general view of scientific explanations was that they were best seen as like deductions from scientific laws. Outside the more theoretical parts of physics, this view is difficult to take seriously. Summarized in a few words, our view is that scientific explanations rest on scientific world views; on what are taken to be the constituents of reality and on what they can do and have done to them. An explanation tells how some of these entities can have acted together to produce the phenomenon to be explained.

It is in part from this conception that we draw our notion of 'entities'. But our notion of entities is also consistent with our assumptions about what constitutes meaning. If meaning is to escape the circle of words pointing to words then it must rest in the end on actions – on what things can do and what can be done to them.

These assumptions are not, of course, things we 'found out'. They crystallize our initial theoretical understandings, and no doubt our prejudices. But at least we can say that in the course of the present work, they did not crack under the strain. Perhaps we can say more – that they proved, at least for us, productive and fruitful, and that in the process they themselves became further enriched.

Results

The problem we set ourselves was to find a way of describing explanations given by teachers in science classrooms. This required us to develop a language to describe such explanations. And that language needed to be firmly based on good empirical data and to have a clear and coherent theoretical basis. It should also be intelligible to and usable by science teachers. This is what we believe we have in fact achieved.

The problem is important because, despite much research attention paid in the past to language in the classroom, and to learning in science, there exists no principled account of what it is to explain science in the classroom. Those who train or advise science teachers have to work wholly from experience, intuition and anecdote. The problem is also important as a difficult case for current theories of communication to deal with, because of the special characteristics of science, notably both the relation of talk and ideas to material reality, and the conceptual distance between students' knowledge and scientific knowledge.

Our results are therefore of two kinds:

- a language for describing explanations in the science classroom, applied to a large number of real examples

• issues and problems for theories of communication more generally which arise out of the distinctive character of science and science classrooms

We will comment on each of these in what follows.

Describing explanations in science

We repeat below from Chapter 1 the main components of our language for describing explanations, and then discuss each briefly:

• scientific explanations understood as analogous to 'stories'
• an account of meaning-making in explanation, itself with four parts:
  creating differences
  constructing entities
  transforming knowledge
  putting meaning into matter
• variation and styles of explanation

We see in scientific explanations an underlying structure analogous to that of a 'story'. There is a world of protagonists (electrons, genes, etc.) which have their proper powers of action. They enact a sequence of events (a current flows, proteins are made). This sequence has an outcome, namely the phenomenon to be explained (a lamp glows, a cell develops). The point of the analogy is that none of these three components can, in science, be taken for granted. Much explanation has to concern the protagonists and the events they enact. Nor may the phenomenon to be explained be at all obvious (e.g. motion of the continents).

For these reasons, we need an account of how teachers create a need for explanation – in communication terms, a difference to be bridged or resolved. Ways of doing so include promises of clarification, eliciting differences of opinion, using stories to suggest ideas, showing counterintuitive results and creating expectations.

Unlike everyday stories, scientific explanations have protagonists unknown to students. Electron, genes and other scientific entities have therefore to be 'talked into existence' for students. This requires explaining what they can do, have done to them and what they are made of. And they will persist, turning up again and again in new and often unexpected contexts, as real things tend to do.

School science is necessarily a carefully versioned form of scientific knowledge, transformed rather than merely 'simplified'. One of our examples analyses the way sound is transformed to become visible in an oscilloscope. Essential to such transformations are analogy and metaphor: the eye as a camera; atomic orbitals as spaces to fill up.

Demonstrations are essential to scientific explanation. Whilst they are usually thought of as 'showing how things are', we show instead that their main function is to invest physical events with special kinds of meaning. They press matter into the service of theory.

Explanations are of many kinds, done in many ways. The features which generate differences between them include their dependence on other explanations, the knowledge, resources and experience of the teacher, the way the classroom work evolves, and the nature of the subject matter. We identify a number of distinctive styles of explanation: activating and using students' knowledge and ideas; encapsulating explanations in stories; enforcing a new vision of 'how things are', and practising using the language appropriate to the explanation.

Explaining as communication

We turn now to look at our framework for describing explanations from a rather wider point of view, seeing it as pointing to issues of importance in communication more generally.

Creating difference

The issue from a communication point of view is how outsiders to fields of theoretical technical and practical competence, can be brought into such a field. Between the science teacher and the science student exists one obvious area of difference, namely knowledge of science. The relevance of this difference is understood by the teacher, but not by the student. The task of teaching is, in a large part, to make that difference known to students, understood by them, and above all, relevant to them: in ordinary parlance, to make science interesting.

'Difference' is also a phenomenon of everyday interactions, but much less visible there. In education, and in science education in particular, this issue appears in sharp form, as there is a clear curriculum, with a set timetable for achieving the aims of that curriculum.

The situational determinants of difference are at least these: the discipline of science, with its various kinds of knowledge; the social institution of 'education' which turn this knowledge into curricula; the student, who is to be inducted into science; and the teacher whose task it is to bring all this together. From the point of view of communication theory it is the relatively clear structure of this situation, and the way the teacher/communicator has continually to adjust what is being done, which proves to be of special interest.

Forms of explanation and meanings of forms

The common sense of linguistics has generally been that there are relatively clear correspondences between form and meaning: a question has an interrogative *form*; a response to an offer is 'yes, please' or 'no, thank you'. Some recent work on scientific discourse, and related work on textual form, has reinforced this common sense through the concept of genre: the form of a scientific report, for example, can be described in relatively clear terms. Some work on textual genres of secondary schools does indeed speak of 'genres of explanation'.

By contrast, we found no fixed formal unit that corresponds to 'an explanation', whether at the level of the clause; or of the sentence or of a sequence of sentences; or in the form of a text with clearly identifiable boundaries. On the contrary, we find that explanations may stretch across whole texts, series of whole texts (as explanatory sequences), or across smaller parts of texts.

We therefore see the unity of explanation *not* as deriving from the *form* of texts or of units of texts, but from patterns of factors which influence explanatory contexts. The textual units which express or realise explanations are quite diverse. Their diversity is to be accounted for in terms of the social and institutional structures of explanatory contexts. Thus we have not arrived at a taxonomy of explanatory forms; but have instead developed a means of describing characteristics of explanatory contexts.

Styles of explanation

One remarkable result is the recognition of a variety of 'styles of explanation'. These 'styles' have their origin in a number of factors. First, there are undeniable differences between teachers, which seem to be the result of personal histories and experience, the effect of the disciplinary issue dealt with, and broad pedagogical and epistemological dispositions training and traditions. All of these interact with – and may be triggered by – characteristics of the class collectively or of individuals in it. So for instance, the use of narrative, 'telling a story', can simultaneously have the multiple functions of establishing rapport, introducing a new topic, and insinuating relevant new knowledge – thus opening the essential difference which prepares for the coming explanatory sequence. Or, eliciting what seems like ordinary, common-sense knowledge from pupils and turning it successively more and more into the form of scientific knowledge, may depend on the suitability of the subject matter, on the teacher's confidence in managing the process, and on an established history of rapport between class and teacher.

'Styles,' however, are not just static, fixed dispositions of individual teachers. In the course of a lesson, there are constant adjustment, changes, shifts, in the form of interaction. So while we can sometimes see a relative stability of style with a particular teacher, and in particular of that teacher with a given class, this stability is not in the least anything like rigidity. We expand on this in the next section.

The dynamics of a multiple communicational environment

Teachers use a range of modes of communication. A sequence may, typically, involve: speech, including the spoken delivery of written language (or 'language for writing down', as in the dictation of bits of curricular knowledge); drawing on the blackboard of diagrams of various levels of complexity; prepared objects used in demonstrating; images from books; gestural forms of delivering information.

It is quite clear from our video-recordings that one has to speak of a multi-semiotic environment, in which language is clearly important, but not solely so or even at times predominantly so. Consequently, there is not only constant adjustment in terms of mode, but there are also constant adjustments in the relative salience of the mode of communication. Teachers are, as it were, playing several instruments, each with its own effects. And they are usually playing harmonies with more than one at a time.

It is important to insist that the various modes each play their part in the construction of entities. The slow pushing movement by the teacher of one hand below the other helps build the theoretical entity 'subduction', as or *more* tellingly than a spoken description. A diagram on the blackboard establishes the entity 'intestine', in the larger structure of entities 'digestive system', as effectively or more effectively than a written description.

Semiotic and conceptual mechanisms and processes

The picture that emerges is one of a constant dynamic: of change of tactics; of shifts between modes of communication; of transformation of knowledge; and of the positioning of students towards knowledge. All these may happen in the slightest, most minute ways, invisible, we feel certain, to either teachers or students, as when a teacher gradually (though the sequence takes barely a minute or so of class time) repositions the perception of members of a class towards the elements of the periodic table. From a '... here *we* have ...' to a 'there are ...' to '... they give ...', 'they like ...', she has completed a movement from personal proximity ('we have' – our electrons, and elements) via an objectively distanced position ('there are ...' in the objective world out there), to an enlivening of that world into active entities ('they give', 'they like').

In the process of teaching, all aspects of the explanatory environment and of its elements are constantly transformed. This has consequences as much for the systems of communication as for the domain of science education: the complex semiotic system is used as the means of managing and producing these transformations. Again, the picture is far removed from one of stable representational systems with these stable resources of representation simply or merely being used: the process is one of constant remaking.

The directionality of these processes is not one way, from material world to its representation. The phenomenon of the *demonstration* in itself shows the connectedness of all elements of this multisemiotic environment. Here the sign-making works in the opposite direction to that generally assumed, which is that the representation 'encodes' an aspect of material reality. On the contrary, in a demonstration an aspect of theoretical reality is 'encoded' by elements of the material reality which is at issue. Reality is made to represent theory; a reversal of what is usually taken to be the semiotic process.

What do we claim?

We do not of course claim that ours is the only way of looking at explanation in the science classroom. But we do claim for it a certain power and generality, which enables us to bring together what are usually thought of as rather disparate parts of the activity of teaching science. Our claim is that our new language of description provides a framework within which we can give accounts of many different ways of explaining; accounts which can bring out similarities and differences between them. We do not claim to have identified every possible kind of explanation. But we do claim that this framework will prove workable and valuable in looking for other ways of explaining, and we can already describe a large number of examples.

The framework we offer is not one from which one can 'read off' how an explanation is going. It does not provide checklists of features. What it does provide are the basic sets of questions which need to be asked in each case, together with a collection of examples of answers on which others can build.

We hope that the framework will prove to be of value in helping teachers and those engaged in their professional development to recognize and reflect on cases of explanation. Simply possessing terms with which to try to describe what one is doing is a big step forward. Naming is half-way to recognizing, and recognizing is half-way to thinking again.

New perspectives in science education

We also claim to have done something new in research in science education. For almost two decades, the main focus of research has been on students' personal understandings. It has yielded valuable and important results. But it has tended to work from an assumption (a particular reading of 'constructivism') that knowledge cannot be 'transmitted' from teacher to student, so that what has to be attended to is the student's own personal construction of knowledge. Our view, stated elsewhere in the book but worth repeating here, is that *communication is action: that to teach is to act on other minds, which act in response.* This makes it worth looking at teaching again, asking what teachers are doing and how they are doing it. We have sought to make *teaching* a topic of research.

Our work is also relatively unusual in combining detailed observation and video-recording of science classrooms, together with a close attention to the subject matter being taught. Many studies have been done using checklists of kinds of interactions; typically these do not record the variety of modes of communication, nor often do they attend much to the subject matter. Many other studies of the language of the classroom have, with exceptions, studied mainly verbal forms of interaction, excluding the many others we have found to be important. They have also been primarily interested, again with some exceptions, not in what is being taught but in the structure and form of relationships in the classroom.

What next?

We conclude the book with some thoughts about what might need to be done next, in research in science education and in research in communication more generally, to follow up the work described here.

What next in science education?

If we have, as we claim, an effective way of describing explanations in the science classroom, then these descriptions can – and need to – be put to use in a variety of ways. They do not tell us what teachers were intending to do, but only what they did, so one important line of inquiry is to see how well teachers' behaviour matches their intentions. More important still, the descriptions do not tell us how the student receives explanations. We need to understand better what counts for students as an explanation, and what they see as the attributes of effective explanations. Only given results of all these kinds will it be possible to answer the seemingly obvious question, 'What explanations work well, when and for whom?' Amongst other things, answering such a question will involve the construction of tests, probes, tasks, resources – call them what you will – to obtain indications of the kind of understandings different explanations may have helped to produce. An obvious direction to pursue here would be asking students to construct explanations themselves, and then to explain their explanations.

A more immediate task, but one of considerable value, would be to see to what extent our language of description of explanations can be understood and used by teachers, in the process of pre-service or in-service training. If it can help teachers to recognize what they are doing, to consider alternatives, and to recognize elements which may be missing from their performance, the work will have served one of its main purposes.

It will also be important to look for ways of extending the analysis from personal interaction in the classroom, to looking at the ways books and material from books play a role in explanation. We did not pursue that line in the present work, because very early on we found two things: first that books were rather little used in science classrooms, and second, that much of their explanatory content was in graphic form. The second finding has led us to new work – now in progress – on graphic communication in science.

What next in studies of communication?

Although we believe that our analysis of explanation is useful and fruitful, it has some important limits which need attention. One is that although we can characterize 'entities' in general terms as having packages of meaning derived from what they can do, what can be done to them, their parts and their membership of clusters and classes, we do not yet have much further analysis of the different kinds of meaning relations which they involve. Thus an entity which is like an autonomously acting physical object looks like a very different package of meaning from either a passive object or a disembodied action. And all these are radically different from entities which are like spaces or places.

Secondly, our treatment of events and processes is perhaps weaker than our treatment of object-like or substance-like entities. They too need an analysis or typology of the kinds just discussed. In both there may be a need to reconsider such basic semantic relations as 'part-of'. 'Red' is a part of white light, and the liver is part of the body, but not obviously in the same sense of 'part-of'.

Our point here is that the field of science education provides an exceptionally fruitful field for the extension of, and challenges to, existing understandings of semiotic theories. In the everyday task of science education, the resources of communication used are wide and varied. The dynamics of that complex environment lead to a constant reshaping of these very same resources of communication: science shapes communication as well as the other way around. That in itself is a challenge to current understandings of communication. A further issue which emerges is the exploration and description of the part played by different modes of communication, and their effects on the production of disciplinary knowledge.

Much of the book has focused on questions of knowledge and understanding. But looked at from another point of view, what is going on in the science classroom changes – or can change – who students *are*. To understand science may change one's subjectivity. We have seen in the book several challenges to students' ideas of themselves – here let the objectification of digestion, in which a comfortable known social process is reconstructed as a biochemical machine, stand for the others.

Finally, science is challenging to theories of meaning-making because of its crucial relation to the material, the physical, the ungainsayable brute material world. Semiotics, with its roots in linguistics, has for good reasons tended to concentrate on meaning-making in language between persons. The actions it grounds meaning in are communicative actions. But science has in addition a component of making sense of physical reality. The student certainly learns science in interaction with a teacher. But the student also constructs explanations in interaction with the physical world (and, of course, began to do this as a baby). We might label this 'material semiosis', as a placeholder for something yet to be understood.

To conclude – an anecdote. Early in the research we observed a class in which a student took off his shoe, put it on a table, tied it to a spring balance, and tried using the spring balance to pull the shoe along the table. At the time we saw but did not record this event, since student and teacher did not communicate, and we assumed there would therefore be little relevance to explanation. But a theory of communication clearly needs to embrace acting so as to build an explanation for oneself. So this example points to yet more work to do.

Appendix

CONTEXT AND SOURCES

Context

In this first section of the appendix we situate the research on which the book is based in its context. A second section provides an annotated bibliography of sources.

Why now?

A perspective from the study of communication

One way of locating an intellectual enterprise is to ask: 'Could this have been done at another time?' We have, in Chapter 1, gratefully acknowledged our use of existing work on language in the science classroom. We think we have gone beyond it in at least two essential respects: we do not think that language is all there is to communicate in science classrooms; and we think that previous work has not been respectful enough of the semiotic import of the practices, objects and activities of science teachers. We think that the science classroom is, in fundamental ways, a different semiotic world to classrooms in geography, history, English. Science, in grappling with the meanings of the material world, produces structures of meaning which are not simply effects of language.

Our approach builds on a long history of revaluing language in social communication. It depends on prior work in many forms of socio-linguistics – in which the names of Basil Bernstein, Dell Hymes and William Labov stand eminently – and of discourse analysis, including particularly that strand known as critical discourse analysis, and in social semiotics, itself announced in Michael Halliday's seminal book *Language as Social Semiotic*.

The collective effort of this work has been to show language as not autonomous, as more diverse, as tied in, everywhere, into social structures and practices, to show language itself as just one social practice, and to point – forcefully – to the fact that other social practices are used to communicate and to make meaning.

A perspective from science education

The past two decades of work in science education have been dominated by two strong traditions: a tradition of emphasizing direct learning of science through practical activity, and the constructivist tradition emphasizing the student's personal construction of knowledge. Whatever their merits – and they have many – these two traditions have combined to draw attention away from the teacher, except as a provider of productive 'learning situations'. Constructivists have rightly been concerned to eradicate the belief that knowledge can be piped from mind to mind. But that does not mean that there is nothing for the teacher to do; no scope for the teacher to seek to act on students' minds. Our focus is thus a shift away from these traditions, bringing attention back to how teachers explain – back in effect to a neglected aspect of rhetoric in the science classroom.

In doing so, we have taken account of many different ways of thinking about 'explanation', ranging from the philosophical to the psychological, taking in on the way explorations of the concept in cognitive science. But we have not tried to add to the number of such interpretations. Rather, we have drawn on them to construct a language for reflecting on explanation in an applied setting – the science classroom.

The work of the project

The data on which the book is based come from an ESRC funded research project 'Explanation in the Science Classroom' (R000234916), undertaken between April 1994 and September 1995 at the University of London Institute of Education.

We began by surveying existing data on classroom talk, examining video-tapes of secondary school science lessons, video-tapes of teacher training sessions, and audio-tapes and transcripts of teachers' discussions of scientific ideas. A small scale survey of currently used secondary school science textbooks was also undertaken. We considered the relationships between diagrams, images and explanation in these books. We first noted here a feature that remained important: that explanations exist on all scales from the whole chapter to a line of text. We used these materials to reach common agreement on what we were looking for and what approaches to use in analysing data.

Having made contact with ten secondary schools in the London area, four were selected and a pilot study was organized and carried out in July 1994 in two of them. Following this, the main study involved 12 teachers in four schools: Swakeley's School for Girls (grant-maintained all-girls comprehensive), North Westminster School (LEA mixed comprehensive), Riddlesdown High School (grant-maintained mixed comprehensive), Harris City Technology College (CTC). The decision to video-record lessons was made as a result of the pilot study: we very quickly found that the teacher's words were by no means the only mode of communication, and sometimes by no means the most important. We found that essential features such as gesture, body movement, pointing, as well as references to blackboard diagrams, computer screens, experimental apparatus, posters and other visual displays, required video rather than the originally planned audio-recording.

The data derive from 52 hours of video tape, of lessons involving all the natural sciences including some earth science. Lessons were recorded from the secondary Years 7 to 10, with one or two from Year 11. The recordings concentrated mainly on the teacher, but were also able to capture some reactions from pupils (including their reactions to the presence of the camera!).

We asked to see ordinary routine lessons, done as they would normally be done. Because we were interested in explanations, we discussed with our teacher colleagues when they were likely to be giving a lesson, or a sequence of lessons, involving a substantial amount of explaining, and selected from what they offered a sample of lessons covering a balanced range of topics across the sciences. In addition to these planned occasions, we collected a few others on the spur of the moment, when we found a teacher about to be doing something of interest. Typically, after recording a session, we had informal discussions with teachers about what they thought had gone on in the lesson. These conversations were not recorded or used as data.

Analysis proceeded by viewing and discussing the tapes and transcripts, developing perspectives from which to analyse them, writing these up and then reconsidering and revising them. The effort was directed to finding 'good' categories with which to describe data, not to exhaustively analysing all the data.

Sources

We provide here a bibliography of works referred to in the book, together with others which may be regarded as the main sources of our ideas and thinking, or which provide alternative or complementary perspectives. We have provided notes on each text to indicate its relationship to our work, and to guide readers who wish to follow up the ideas.

Antaki, C. (ed.) (1988) *Analysing Everyday Explanation*. London: Sage.
> This collection of studies of different ways to account for explanation in various social settings draws on a number of disciplinary backgrounds, including social psychology, linguistics, discourse analysis and artificial intelligence. Amongst the many insights offered are a challenge to the idea that explanation is about statements expressing causality, and evidence of the unreliability of linguistic markers (such as 'because') to identify explanations in discourse (see especially the chapter by Draper).

Antaki, C. (1994) *Explaining and Arguing: The Social Organisation of Accounts*. London: Sage.
> The concern here is with everyday explanation and argument, seen from the standpoint of 'discursive psychology' in which discourse is understood as action.

Bhaskar, R. (1978) *A Realist Theory of Science*. London: Harvester Wheatsheaf.
> Bhaskar provides here a defence of realism in the philosophy of science. One important contribution is the identification of what he calls 'the epistemic fallacy': that what exists is reducible to what we know.

Edwards, D. and Mercer, N. (1987) *Common Knowledge: The Development of Understanding in the Classroom*. London: Methuen.
> Coming from a background of social psychology, Edwards and Mercer interpret the process of teaching as a movement towards common knowledge occurring between teacher and student. They consider a wide variety of school subjects, and so do not focus primarily on school science. Their transcripts, and arguments, are attentive to the interaction of language, action and images. They represent the educational process as ideological and founded on asymmetries of power, and in this to be distinguished from

non-educational communication. They provide a forceful discussion of the specific features of classroom interaction, the relationship of those features to social relations, and their sometimes harmful impact on learning. Their position leans more to Vygotsky than to Piaget.

Halliday, M.A.K. (1978) *Language as Social Semiotic*. London: Edward Arnold.
This seminal work is now old, but not at all outdated. Although challenging to linguists it is not technical in nature and is accessible to the non-linguist reader. It in several places has an explicit focus on education, but its main merit is its wide but deeply thought-through perspective on language as one aspect of what it is to be a social being.

Halliday, M.A.K. (1985) *An Introduction to Functional Grammar*. London: Edward Arnold.
Our work in this project has been fundamentally shaped by systemic functional linguistics, which is a functionally oriented linguistics linking grammatical forms to social situations. That theory has provided much of the backdrop to our analysis. The book is fundamentally a handbook of linguistic analysis, and not readily accessible to non-linguists. It offers a comprehensive account of language, with many essential insights into the multiple tasks which language performs simultaneously.

Halliday, M.A.K. and Martin, J.R. (1993) *Writing Science*. London: Falmer Press.
Writing Science is a collection of articles on science texts from a systemic functional linguistics perspective. The focus is on language in written texts. The analyses identify features of the language of science proper and of science textbooks, and characterize some significant text-types (genres) of science, providing considerable insights into the language of science, the language of science classrooms, and how language works generally. A number of the articles contrast science language with the language of other subject areas.

Harré, R. (1985) *Varieties of Realism*. Oxford: Blackwell.
Harré promotes a view of the scientific enterprise as a cluster of material and cognitive practices whose participants are bound by moral commitments. Important contributions of the book include the account of analogical explanations in science, the idea of 'policy realism', and the analysis of the different roles played by entities in explanations according to their degree of accessibility to experience.

Hempel, C.G. (1965) *Aspects of Scientific Explanation*. London: The Free Press.
We include this text as representative of philosophical accounts of explanation. Hempel develops the logical positivist philosophy of science to generate a 'logic of scientific explanation'. An explanation is seen as a deduction of phenomena from axioms which include at least one general law. Such accounts mainly aim to formulate logically necessary and sufficient conditions for something to be an explanation. See also Lipton (1991).

Hodge, R. and Kress, G. (1988) *Language as Ideology* (2nd edn). London: Routledge.
The book, first published in 1979, attempts to relate the grammar of English to the social, economical and cultural organizations of society at a particular time. It is set within the functional theory of language of Michael Halliday, but uses linguistic concepts from other theories, notably the concept of transformation. It provides detailed analyses of a variety of texts.

Hodge, R. and Kress, G. (1989) *Social Semiotics*. Cambridge: Polity Press.
This book extends functional theories of language and communication to a wide range of modes and media of communication: images, sculpture, family structures and narratives, language, spatial organizations, fashion, comics, films, advertisement, and so on. It provides detailed descriptions of the organization, effects, and social uses of these forms.

Johnson, M. (1987) *The Body in the Mind: The Bodily Basis of Meaning, Imagination and Reason*. Chicago: University of Chicago Press.

> An ambitious attempt to construct a theory of meaning and of rationality which grounds them in human actions and bodily experience.

Kress, G. and van Leeuwen, T. (1996) *Reading Images: A Grammar of Visual Design*. London: Routledge.

> *Reading Images* provides a semantically oriented analysis of images. It offers an understanding of how language and images may complement each other and interact. The description and classification of images also considers their communicational characteristics, and the relationship of images to cultural, social and technological change. The scope of the book is broad, and so the attention to science images is limited, but with potential for development.

Lakoff, G. and Johnson, M. (1980) *Metaphors We Live By*. Chicago: University of Chicago Press.

> Lakoff and Johnson argue that metaphors lie at the roots of our conceptualization and understanding of the world. Their pervasive character in both cognition and communication, as well as their grounding in bodily experience, are illustrated by a wealth of examples throughout the book.

Lakoff, G. (1987) *Women, Fire and Dangerous Things*. Chicago: Chicago University Press.

> This long book elaborates and defends Lakoff's view of language as founded on metaphor. Much of the book is taken up with a critical analysis of classical views which he rejects.

Lemke, J.L. (1990) *Talking Science: Language, Learning and Values*. Norwood, New Jersey: Ablex.

> *Talking Science* is based on research into the secondary science classroom. The analyses have a linguistic orientation, based on long passages of carefully analysed transcript, with a particularly strong discussion of the semantic relations of the school-subject science, which he calls 'thematic patterns'. The analyses show how science content may be extracted from classroom talk. The process of learning is largely construed as the student approximating to the 'science way of talking' as produced by the teacher, rather than as a transformation of the student's way of thinking. *Talking Science* is informed by social theory, and science learning is located within social relations of authority.

Lipton, P. (1991) *Inference to the Best Explanation*. London: Routledge.

> This short but wide-ranging text offers descriptions of the main philosophical accounts of scientific inference and explanation, and provides a select but up to date bibliography for those wanting to read further.

Martin, J.R. (1992) *English Text: System and Structure*. Amsterdam: Benjamin.

> *English Text* presents a set of techniques for the analysis of extended passages of discourse, along with a careful and detailed discussion of the specific relationships between language features and social situations, within a systemic linguistics framework.

Ogborn, J. (1994) Theoretical and Empirical Investigations of the Nature of Scientific and Common-sense Knowledge. PhD thesis, University of London.

> An extended account of the theorizing about explanation used in our book is to be found here. The work includes in addition empirical studies of the basic dimensions of common-sense reasoning about the physical world, results of which have informed our analyses.

Ogborn, J. (1995) 'Recovering reality'. *Studies in Science Education*, Vol. 25, pp. 3–38.

> This long review paper offers a stout defence of realism in science, founded

on the notion of a scientific ontology of entities, which participate in explanation. It attacks those who draw anti-realist conclusions from recent work in the sociology of scientific knowledge.

Ortony, A. (1979) *Metaphor and Thought*. Cambridge: Cambridge University Press.
This old, but recently reprinted collection is still useful. It offers a variety of perspectives on metaphor from philosophical, linguistic and other points of view.

Piaget, J. and Garcia, R. (1987) *Vers une Logique des Significations*. Geneva: Murionde. (Translated 1991, *Toward a Logic of Meaning*. New Jersey: Lawrence Erlbaum.)
Together with Piaget's earlier work, which develops the idea that thoughts have origin in *internalized actions* and reality is *constructed*, not given, this posthumously published book has been a valuable source for our work. The book offers an account of how meanings of entities are constructed through action, through what they can do, what you can do to them and what they are made of.

Rosch, E. and Lloyd, B.B. (1978) *Cognition and Categorization*. New Jersey: Lawrence Erlbaum.
This book is important as an early source of the idea that human categories of physical things are based on prototypes rather than on necessary and sufficient conditions. This makes space for reasoning by similarity, analogy and metaphor.

Schank, R. (1986) *Explanation Patterns*. New Jersey: Lawrence Erlbaum Associates.
From a cognitive science perspective, Schank attempts to see how the creative making of an explanation could be done mechanically, and in the process furnishes a variety of concepts which are useful in analysing explanations. He offers useful ideas about different levels of need for explanation, and a point of view in which explanation and memory are linked as driven by failures of expectation.

Sinclair, J. Mc.H. and Coulthard, R.M. (1975) *Towards an Analysis of Discourse*. London: Oxford University Press.
An early and influential example of analysis of classroom discourse, which happened to be based substantially on lessons in science. It introduces the 'question–response–evaluation' triad.

Sutton, C. (1992) *Words, Science and Learning*. Buckingham: Open University Press.
In this book, Clive Sutton continues and develops his previous work on language in science. He chooses to focus on words, and at this simple level, brings out the rich and imaginative substructure that scientific terms carry. The book pleads for a much stronger focus in science education on imagination and interpretation.

Vosniadou, S. and Ortony, A. (1989) *Similarity and Analogical Reasoning*, Cambridge: Cambridge University Press.
This collection of articles on metaphor and analogy ranges widely over the cognitive disciplines, and offers a variety of interesting, often incompatible, points of view.

INDEX